NAT TURNER

• and the •

SOUTHAMPTON REVOLT of 1831

MARTIN S. GOLDMAN

An Impact Biography

Franklin Watts
New York   London   Toronto   Sydney

Maps by Vantage Art
Insert photographs copyright © : Virginia State Library and Archives,
Photographic Services, Richmond, VA: pp. 3, 8, 16; North Wind Picture
Archives: pp. 1 top, 4, 5, 9 bottom, 12, 13, 14, 15; The Bettmann Archive:
pp. 1 bottom, 2 top, 6, 9 top, 10; Nawrocki Stock Photo, Chicago, IL: p. 7;
Historical Pictures Service, Chicago, IL: p. 2 bottom; Culver Pictures: p. 11.

Library of Congress Cataloging in Publication Data

Goldman, Martin S.
Nat Turner and the Southampton revolt of 1831 / by Martin S. Goldman.
p.   cm. — (An Impact biography)
Includes bibliographical references and index.
Summary: Describes the life of the slave and preacher who led the most
successful slave rebellion in American history.
ISBN 0-531-13011-8
1. Southampton Insurrection, 1831—Juvenile literature.   2. Turner, Nat,
1800?-1831—Juvenile literature.   3. Slaves-Virginia—Southampton
County—Biography—Juvenile literature.   4. Southampton County
(Va.)–Biography—Juvenile literature.
[1. Turner, Nat, 1800?-1831.   2. Slaves.   3. Afro-Americans-Biography.
4. Southampton Insurrection, 1831.]   I. Title.
F232.s7G65   1992
975.5'5503'092—DC20   91-36618 CIP AC

Contents

To my mother and father,
Ruth and Louis Goldman

He stood erect; his eyes flashed fire;
His robust form convulsed with ire;
"I will be free! I will be free!
Or fighting, die a man!" cried he.

Virginia's hills were lit at night—
The slave had risen in his might.
And far and near Nat's wail went forth,
To South and East, and West and North....

—T. Thomas Fortune,
from a poem published in the
Cleveland Gazette, November 22, 1884

Introduction
The Search for Nat Turner

Nat Turner, an American slave, has been largely forgotten in the pages of American history—even by the vast majority of African-Americans. Who was Nat Turner, and what is his rightful place in the American past? To find the remnants of Nat Turner and his world we must return to the first three decades of the nineteenth century. There we can reconstruct the meaningful story of one of the few instances of organized armed resistance to what historians still call "the peculiar institution"—American slavery.

Despite the fact that he organized and led the most successful slave rebellion in American history, the real Nat Turner remains shrouded in myth and mystery. And yet, in the years before the Civil War, no American slave could match Turner's impact on the institution of slavery. As news of the Turner slave rebellion in 1831 spread from Southampton, Virginia, throughout the slave South, the southern heart, like that of the biblical pharaoh who repeatedly refused

7

the pleas of Moses to free the Hebrew slaves in Egypt, hardened in its overt and public defense of slavery.

The Turner rebellion brought a reaction that lasted until the great Civil War ultimately decided the fate of slavery in the United States. The immediate result of the uprising led by the mysterious slave-preacher known as "The Prophet" was to promote fear and dread, even among nonslaveholding whites, of slave revolutions throughout the heartland of the Old South.

As historian Kenneth M. Stampp has written, "No ante-bellum [pre–Civil War] Southerner could ever forget Nat Turner. The career of this man made an impact upon the people of this section as great as that of John C. Calhoun or Jefferson Davis."[1]

Indeed, after 1831, many southern plantation mothers would frighten their misbehaving children with midnight tales and scary stories about "Old Nat." Clearly, the "spirit of Nat" was a major theme that struck familiar chords of fear and terror time and again in the hearts and minds of slaveowners from Virginia to the deep South in the three decades before the Civil War.[2]

The historical record is sparse. On November 1, 1831, the day after his capture, Nat Turner was questioned by a local attorney, Thomas R. Gray. While rumors and exaggerations swept through the South, the authorities were anxious to get the facts of the Turner rebellion out to a deeply troubled southern public.

Accordingly, Gray visited Turner and, as far as can be determined, recorded *The Confessions of Nat Turner, the Leader of the Late Insurrection in Southampton, Va. As fully and voluntarily made to Thomas R. Gray....* By the end of November 1831, thousands of copies of the famous *Confessions* were being read all over the South. However, the pamphlet was quickly suppressed, and many copies were destroyed. Few survive today. As one Virginia news-

8

paper angrily stated, "Too much importance has already been given to the miserable wretch."[3] Others worried that distribution of Turner's *Confessions* would incite other slaves to rise up against their masters in other parts of the Old South.

Most historians believe that the Gray pamphlet is authentic. Attorney Gray was a white slaveholder, and Nat Turner's words are filtered through the narrow prism of Gray's obviously biased interpretation. But there is little argument today that the Gray pamphlet contradicts the other available published newspaper accounts of the famous slave rebellion. More important, according to the testimony of a number of persons who were present when the Gray pamphlet was read back to him, Turner himself stated that it was a "full, free and voluntary" testimony.[4]

After the Civil War, the Nat Turner story quietly receded into the overlooked pages of African-American history. In most U.S. history textbooks used in high schools or colleges, Nat Turner rarely got more than a few lines when the issues of slavery or slave rebellions before the Civil War were discussed. For example, one of the most widely read college texts used during the 1950s and 1960s was *The Growth of the American Republic*, by Samuel Eliot Morison and Henry Steele Commager. Only six lines in that book, plus a passing mention in two chapters dealing with the southern states and the abolition movement, were devoted to the saga of Turner's rebellion.[5]

Even a specialized study like Avery Craven's *The Coming of the Civil War* paid little attention to the role that Nat Turner played on the stage of American history. It merely credited the Turner rebellion with hastening the debate over slavery in the Virginia Assembly during 1832.

Harriet Beecher Stowe used Nat Turner as the model for the hero of her 1856 sequel to *Uncle Tom's Cabin*, which she titled *Dred: A Tale of the Dismal*

Swamp. Dred is a runaway slave who identifies with the Hebrew prophets and delivers endless tirades against slavery. The novel, meant to depict the evils of slavery, has among its characters a brutal master who ultimately goads the slaves into rebellion.[6]

However, despite momentary revivals, little was heard about the elusive Nat Turner for almost a century. As the years passed, there were exceptions, of course, to the historical oversight that neglected Nat Turner in telling the story of America's past. But these exceptions rarely filtered into the classrooms of most twentieth-century American students. The Nat Turner rebellion was almost never taught. As the slave South had hoped in 1831, the man has been largely forgotten except by a few obscure scholars.

Where does the controversy over Nat Turner's place in American history leave us? After more than 160 years, we still wonder what really happened in Southampton County, Virginia, back in the late summer of 1831. No plaque or marker exists to commemorate the Nat Turner revolt. A sign that once stood on Highway 58 in Southampton County was removed. Virginia's state and local authorities, even today, do not want to remind anyone that Nat Turner ever lived. Yet there are still those who cannot and will not forget. There are still those in search of the real Nat Turner and the important meaning and legacy of his bloody rebellion—a rebellion that served to change the course of American history in the three decades before the Civil War.

Nat Turner Grows Up a Slave

...my uncommon intelligence for a child, remarked I had too much sense to be raised, and if I was, I would never be any service to anyone as a slave.

—Nat Turner,
from his *Confessions*

On October 2, 1800, the same year Thomas Jefferson, a Virginia planter and slaveowner, was elected third president of the United States, Nat Turner was born into slavery. Nat was born on the modest plantation of Benjamin Turner in Southampton County, Virginia, almost 70 miles (113 km) southeast of Richmond. Like most American slaves, he took the last name of his master.

The Turner plantation was a large farm, sprawled over several hundred acres on Rosa Swamp, that produced tobacco, corn, apples, and cotton. Carved out of the Virginia wilderness over three generations, the Turner plantation wasn't nearly as grand as Scarlett

O'Hara's fictional Tara plantation in the novel *Gone With the Wind* (elegantly described by the author, Margaret Mitchell, as "a whitewashed brick plantation house" that was "an island set in a wild red sea" of dogwoods and pink peach blossoms).[1]

It had a two-story house that was probably typical of the modest homes of most southern slaveowners, "just a box, with four rooms, bisected by a hallway, and a detached kitchen at the back. Wind-swept in winter, it was difficult to keep clean of vermin in summer. But it was huge, it had great white columns in front, and it was eventually painted white, and so, in this land of wide fields and pinewoods it seemed very imposing."[2]

The county seat of Southampton was Jerusalem, a town by the Nottoway River. About two thousand people lived there, some 50 to 60 miles (81 to 97 km) from the prospering city of Norfolk on the Atlantic Ocean. When Nat Turner was born, the region—dotted with farms, plantations, and sleepy villages along the North Carolina border—was, in many respects, hardly removed from the frontier. As one of the South's great twentieth-century writers, Wilbur J. Cash, observed about Virginia and the Old South in which Nat Turner grew up, "The land had to be wrestled from the forest and the intractable red man. It was a harsh and bloody task.... The inference is plain. It is impossible to conceive the great South as being, on the whole, more than a few steps removed from the frontier stage."[3]

Thus, the world of Virginia that Nat Turner found all about him, as the child of slaves, was one of great instability. As he ran about the Turner plantation, a happy youngster playing with the other children—the white children of his master and the black children of the other slaves—young Nat must have become gradually aware that sometime soon he would be forced to be different from the white chil-

12

dren. Like all of the other slave children who took their meals and slept in the crude cabins that made up the slave quarters, little Nat knew that the time would come when he would be forced to separate from his white playmates. Then he would take his place, like the generations of black slaves before him, at the bottom of southern society. On the Turner plantation, Nat Turner would become another piece of property on a growing farm in the Virginia backwoods. Such an unsettling fact of life had to weigh heavily on the developing mind of an intelligent and sensitive youngster.

Although born a slave, Nat always felt he was special. He recalled playing with the other children on the farm when he was three or four years old. It was then, Turner related, "I was telling them something, which my mother overhearing, said it happened before I was born.... I surely would be a prophet, as the Lord had shewn [sic] me things that had happened before my birth. And my father and mother strengthened me in this my first impression, saying in my presence, I was intended for some great purpose."[4]

Others agreed. Nat recalled:

My grandmother, who was very religious and to whom I was much attached—my master, who belonged to the church, and other religious persons who visited the house, and whom I often saw at prayers, noticing the singularity of my manners, I suppose, and my uncommon intelligence for a child, remarked I had too much sense to be raised, and if I was, I would never be any service to anyone as a slave.[5]

As Nat Turner passed those steamy and happy summers of his childhood swimming, fishing, trapping, or playing all of the wonderful games that children love to play, the surface of that tranquil world appeared to be happy and peaceful. But the visible appearance of the serenity of life in the Old South was cunningly deceptive. Beneath the peaceful exterior of southern life lay a tradition of unrest and violence. The South teetered on the institution of human slavery, which had become the linchpin of its life and culture over the previous two centuries. Virginia was a repressive society in which tight controls restricted the freedoms of free blacks as well as slaves. Underneath the surface of what appeared to be a tranquil world of elegant ladies and dashing gentlemen farmers festered a society in which brutality was a daily occurrence. Amid the Old South's moonlight and magnolias there was the capacity for great violence.

As a youngster, little Nat was especially friendly with John Clark Turner, one of the three sons of his masters, a boy close to his age. A more important influence on the young slave was his grandmother. A withered and gnarled woman who was apparently too old to do physical work around the Turner plantation, Nat's grandmother, Old Bridget, would tell her grandson folktales about slaves and stories from the Bible. The Turners were devout Methodists and did their utmost to steep their thirty-some slaves in Christian belief and teachings by holding prayer services on the farm and by taking their slaves to church on Sunday.

Little is known of Nat's father, not even his name. But Nat's mother, Nancy, was said to be a large, olive-skinned African woman who had been brought to America before 1808—one of 15 million native Africans estimated to have been kidnapped or stolen from their motherland after 1619.

The African slave trade, for many years the subject of much opposition by antislavery groups and free blacks because of its inherent brutality and inhumanity, was finally abolished in the United States in 1808. However, by that time there were approximately 1 million slaves in the United States, whose children would serve to replenish the dwindling stock of Africans. Most slaves taken from Africa never reached the United States. They ended up in either the Caribbean area or Latin America. However, some Americans continued to engage illegally in the very profitable slave trade until after the War of 1812.

Unlike many American Negro slaves who came from the agricultural tribes along the West Coast of Africa, Nat Turner's mother was from the northern Nile River country in central Africa. Nancy had been kidnapped as a teenager and was forced to march the long distance to the west coast. Branded and sold to European slave traders, Nancy found herself on a crowded slave ship. She underwent the dreaded Middle Passage—the heartless and grueling trip to the New World, where Africans died by the millions over two centuries of the cruel slave trade.

No one will ever know exactly how many Africans were brought to the New World by the slave traders, but one thing is certain. The Middle Passage—which took six to eight weeks depending on the port of destination—was a horror. As John Hope Franklin points out, "Overcrowding was common.... More slaves meant greater profits, and few traders could resist the temptation to wedge in a few more. There was hardly standing, lying, or sitting room. Chained together by twos, hands and feet, the slaves had no room in which to move about and no freedom to exercise their bodies even in the slightest."[6]

As many as half of the slaves shipped from Africa died from either starvation, suicide, or a dread disease such as smallpox or influenza. Nat Turner's mother is said to have landed in Norfolk, Virginia, in 1795. From Norfolk, she was marched inland in a long chained line of slaves called a coffle. Sometime in 1799, Benjamin Turner purchased the young African woman and took her to his growing plantation in

Southampton County. Soon after, she married one of Old Bridget's sons. Later generations claimed that Nat Turner's mother was of royal African blood. Such claims, however, possibly owe more to the legends that sprang up around Nat Turner in the years after his death than they do to historical fact.[7]

Growing up on the Turner plantation, young Nat Turner displayed a remarkable talent for learning. Since it is highly doubtful that Nat's parents were literate, no one to this day knows who taught the youngster to read and write. Yet young Nat, whose biblical name Nathaniel meant "the gift of God," constantly amazed the other slaves with his knowledge. Nat recalled, "The manner in which I learned to read and write, not only had great influence on my own mind, as I acquired it with the most perfect ease, so much so, that I have no recollection whatever of learning the alphabet."

One day a slave gave Nat a book to keep him from crying. He immediately began spelling out the names of many of the objects that were pictured in the pages of the book. Both of his parents were proud of him and showered him with praise. Their child, they told the other slaves, was destined for greatness. They proudly showed the other slaves that Nat had bumps and scars on his head and on his chest. In Africa, males who bore such markings were by tradition destined for leadership. "I was intended for some great purpose," Nat said.

Everyone who watched the little boy grow up in the Turner slave quarters became convinced that he was marked for greatness. In his *Confessions*, Nat says that when he was no more than three or four years old his parents were already certain that one day he "surely would be a prophet."[8]

Nat emerged as a leader among his playmates. When they would go off into the woods to sabotage animal traps by releasing the animals or to steal goodies from neighboring plantations, Nat would often be the one to lead them. But he was careful not to steal anything himself. It wouldn't do for a future prophet to be branded with the label of a common thief. By choice, Nat Turner led an austere life, and he became increasingly mysterious to his playmates and to the curious adults who watched him grow up. Wrapping himself in religious mysticism, which those who knew him felt was inspired by God, Nat Turner grew up supremely confident that one day he would be a leader of his people. And so he chose a path that would make him stand out while at the same time cloak him in mystery. As he said, "Having soon discovered to be great, I must appear so, and therefore studiously avoided mixing in society, and wrapped myself in mystery, devoting myself to fasting and prayer."

As he approached the time when he would be old enough to work around the Turner farm, Nat took the opportunity to spend much of his free time reading and thinking. As the years passed, he steeped himself in books and religion. Unlike most slaves, who were forbidden to learn to read and write, Nat Turner loved books.

"Whenever an opportunity occurred of looking at a book, when the school children were out getting their lessons, I would find many things that the fertility of my own imagination had depicted to me before; all my time, not devoted to my master's service, was spent either in prayer, or in making experiments," Nat remembered years later.[9]

In 1809, when Nat was nine years old, Benjamin Turner's oldest son, Samuel, bought 360 acres (144 hectares) from his father. Located 2 miles (3 km) south of the Turner plantation, Samuel Turner's land needed slaves to work the cotton fields. Benjamin Turner lent his son eight slaves. Among them were Nat and his mother. Sometime before this, Nat's father had run away. He found slavery so oppressive

17

that he was willing to leave his wife and child for the freedom of the North. He was willing to risk a severe beating, at the very least, if caught. Rumor had it that he ended up in the African nation of Liberia. Wherever he went, Nat's father was never seen again in Southampton County.

In 1810, Nat's master, Benjamin Turner died in a typhoid epidemic. Soon thereafter his wife, Elizabeth, also became ill and died. In his will, Benjamin Turner divided his land and his slaves between his three surviving children. Nat, his mother, and his grandmother then became the legal property of Samuel Turner.

When he reached the age of twelve, the world changed for young Nat. Because he was now expected to work as a slave, Nat was no longer permitted to play with the white children. He watched from the fields as his childhood friends went off to fine schools and academies. The full force of who and what he was must have troubled the mind of such a bright youngster. Despite his intelligence and despite the fact that he was regarded as "special" by whites and blacks alike, Nat Turner was a slave. His childhood ended abruptly when he was forced to work the fields with the other field hands on Samuel Turner's small farm. For the sensitive and intelligent boy, this initial encounter with the pain and reality of slavery was a shock that was to have a profound influence on his life.

Nat's days were hard and long. He awakened before the crack of dawn, ate a simple breakfast of mixed grains called cornpone and mush, milked the cows, and fed the chickens and pigs. At first light, after the blowing of the horn that ordered the field hands into the field, he would toil at backbreaking work until dusk. The slaves spent the late winter and spring planting cotton. In the hot and steamy summers, they would hoe the cotton sprouts, all the while battling the fierce mosquitoes and gnats that relentlessly preyed on them from the nearby woods and insect-infested swamps.

When the sun was high, the slaves would be permitted a dinner break. Some cornmeal, bacon fat, or salted pork was brought to them from the slave quarters. During the break they would talk, sing, or nap until the driver hired by Samuel Turner to direct the work of the slaves prodded them to get back to work. In the late afternoon the slaves would return to their hoeing, pick the worms from the cotton plants, or work in the nearby fields sowing corn or tobacco.

Though under the intense oppression of a cruel institution that could break up slave family life without a moment's warning, the slaves somehow managed to fill their difficult lives with a small measure of contentment. Slave life, while often severe, had its quiet and peaceful moments. In the privacy of their cabins the slaves could gather around the warmth of the fireplace after supper and tell stories, sing songs, and dream the dreams that all human beings cherish. The slaves could also visit their neighbors in nearby cabins and pass the time catching up on local gossip or the latest news from town. Slaves courted, fell in love, married by their own rituals, and raised families.

Samuel Turner, though a harsher master than his father, was smart enough to allow his slaves to attend Sunday prayer meetings, where Master Turner's brand of Christianity served a dual purpose. The Bible was used by the South's master class to save the unconverted heathen souls and at the same time indelibly imprint the fact that God Almighty wanted Negroes to be slaves; that slavery was their proper station in life. The white preachers invariably preached that a better life awaited the slaves in their next world, the kingdom of heaven.

After the Sunday prayer meeting the slaves were generally free to hold their own separate prayer groups, dances, and picnics. Also, many slaves were permitted to work a little patch by their cabins, where they could raise collards, peas, and sweet potatoes for holiday meals. Slaves were usually permitted a four-day holiday at Christmas, a week off after the harvest, and a day each on Easter and on the Fourth of July. If a slave was thrifty and worked his truck garden carefully, he might even save enough money from selling his produce for a jug of whiskey for the holidays (getting drunk was an accepted part of any holiday celebration.)[10]

Nat Turner, however, had no time for the little frivolities and leisure of slave life on Samuel Turner's farm. Nat never drank; he preferred to spend his time reading or in prayer. As he recalled those early slave years:

...I reverted in my mind to the remarks made of me in my childhood, and the things that had been shewn [sic] me—and as it had been said of me in my childhood by those by whom I had been taught to pray, both white and black, and in whom I had the greatest confidence, that I had too much sense to be raised, and if I was, I would never be of any use to any one as a slave.[11]

So Nat Turner passed those crucial years of his early young manhood, working long, hard hours, watching, learning, and waiting.

2

Nat Turner's World: Slavery in Virginia (1800–1830)

*...this momentous question, like a fire-bell in the
night, awakened and filled me with terror. I
considered it at once as the knell of the Union. It is
hushed, indeed, for the moment. But this is a reprieve
only.... We have the wolf by the ears, and we can
neither hold him, nor safely let him go.*

—Thomas Jefferson, 1820
writing on slavery in the
new territories of the United States

Slavery had existed since ancient times. When the
Western world introduced slavery in the fifteenth and
sixteenth centuries, it was not a modern institution. In
fact, slavery had existed in the earliest known history
of Africa, where, in some parts of the continent, there
was no racial basis for turning your enemies into servants for life. The ancient Egyptians enslaved the people they captured in wars, as did the Greeks and
Romans. When Muslims invaded Africa, they seized

women for their harems and men for their armies and to serve them as laborers.

The modern institution of slavery was created when the spirit of the Renaissance collided head-on with the forces of modern commerce. The Renaissance produced the philosophy that people were free to pursue pleasure. Thus, they had the liberty to destroy freedom or to exploit other human beings. Parallel to the rise of powerful European nation-states like Spain, France, Portugal, and Great Britain, a revolution in commerce enabled these states to reap great national treasure as they fiercely competed with one another in the trading of human beings for profit.[1]

The first slaves were brought to the American colonies in 1619, when a Dutch ship sold twenty Africans to the English colonist John Rolfe in Virginia. Slavery quickly adapted itself to the cultivation of tobacco in the Virginia colony where, during the early period, the African slaves worked side by side with white workers and servants on the growing plantations and small farms. In fact, during the sixteenth and seventeenth centuries the English, Dutch, Spaniards, and Portuguese were quick to use slave labor and held Indians and whites in bondage as well as Africans.

The roots of Virginia slavery ran deep in the nation's history. For about twenty years, between 1619 and the 1640s, Virginia's laws did not discriminate between the races. However, it was clear that by the 1640s owners of Negro slaves began holding them and their children for "life and perpetuity." One historian believes that the fact that black slaves were selling for twice the price of white indentured servants was a clear indication that the growing master class saw blacks as slaves for life, whereas whites were gradually able to work off their period of indentured servitude. By the 1660s the Virginia colony was passing laws that clearly defined slavery along racial terms. For example, in 1662 a law stated that "whereas some doubts have arisen whether children got by any Englishman upon a negro woman shall be slave or free...all children born in this colony shall be bond [slave] or free only according to the condition of the mother."[2]

Thus, slavery was recognized and established as *hereditary* (passing from parents to children) in Virginia law. Only eighteen years later, in 1680, the Virginia colony passed police laws to control and restrict the daily lives of the growing slave population.

Such pieces of legislation, deeply rooted in the fabric of Virginia colonial life, easily survived as Virginia went from colony to statehood following the American Revolution. By 1800, the year Nat Turner was born, blacks numbered almost half of Virginia's population, and white slaveholders grew increasingly concerned about the growing danger of slave dissatisfaction and unrest in their midst. By Turner's time there had been few real uprisings, but still the slaveholders were uneasy with the presence of so many bondsmen living among them. The whites clearly had cause to worry. They did so because slavery, even under the best conditions, was a brutal and degrading way of life.

In the northern states, slavery was gradually made illegal during the 1780s. Northerners may not have agreed on the question of whether or not slavery was profitable, but they could not argue with the notion that the principles of the American Revolution did not apply to blacks. A system of gradual emancipation in the North took place over about a generation.

But the South was a different place. As the North became more hostile toward slavery, the southerners, who were far more isolated and little removed from the frontier, found themselves increasingly defending their "peculiar institution." After all, even President Thomas Jefferson was a slaveholder. Although he personally disliked slavery, none of his slaves was freed until after he died. Even then, because of heavy debt, only five slaves were set free.[3]

Jefferson was clearly uncomfortable with slavery. In 1774 the young revolutionary sent his friend Patrick Henry a copy of an untitled paper, which was later published in Philadelphia and London. Widely read throughout the British colonial empire, Jefferson's "Summary View of the Rights of British America" (as it came to be called) contained an unequivocal attack on slavery: "The abolition of domestic slavery is the great object of desire in those [American] colonies, where it was, unhappily, introduced in their infant state. But previous to the enfranchisement of the slaves we have, it is necessary to exclude all further importations from Africa."[4]

In his initial draft of the Declaration of Independence, Jefferson had attacked England's King George III for his refusal to end the slave trade. He accused the king of conducting a "cruel war against human nature...captivating & carrying them into slavery in another hemisphere or to insure miserable death in their transportation hither." The passage was cut out when delegates from South Carolina and Georgia complained. By 1784, a year after the American Revolution ended successfully, Jefferson had returned home to serve in the Virginia legislature. There he led the fight to exclude slavery from newly created states that were certain to be formed as the new nation expanded. As Fawn Brodie notes in her biography of Jefferson, "No single legislative proposal in American history had so much promise for preventing future mischief from escalating into calamity. But southern delegates swarmed to protest with invective of singular violence."[5]

Jefferson's resolution lost by the vote of a single delegate. Had it succeeded, the South and slavery would have been isolated quite early in the country's history as the northern state legislatures were sweeping slavery off the books by statute.

Earlier, Jefferson had written in his famous *Notes on the State of Virginia*, that blacks should be sent back to Africa, where they had originated. But by the end of his life Jefferson came to realize that colonization was unworkable. He believed that the spread of slavery into the new states that would soon be carved out of the West and Southwest would bring the nation certain future trouble. Thus, he did everything he could to stop the spread of slavery as the nation developed.

In 1785, Jefferson replaced Benjamin Franklin as minister to France. In 1787, Jefferson was in Paris when he learned that his beloved Virginia had finally suspended the slave trade. Writing a note of congratulation to a friend back home, Jefferson rejoiced that the slave trade in Virginia had ended, pointing out that "this abomination must have an end, and there is a superior bench reserved in heaven for those who hasten it."[6]

When Jefferson became president of the United States in 1801, he continued his attack on the Atlantic slave trade by making its prohibition part of his legislative program. In his annual message to Congress in 1806, Jefferson supported legislation that would finally bring the hated trade in human beings to an end.

The bill passed, but not without strong congressional opposition that hinted at trouble in the future should any president attempt to outlaw the extension of slavery. For a time there was even talk of secession as southern lawmakers threatened to pull their states out of the Union. Clearly, feelings about slavery ran deep.

The bill prohibiting the Atlantic slave trade provided a fine of $20,000, a considerable fortune in those days, and forfeiture of any ship equipped for the brutal slave trade. In addition, there was a fine of from

$1,000 to $10,000, with imprisonment of from five to ten years, for anyone caught by the authorities transporting or selling slaves on the Atlantic Ocean. Even though South Carolina was the only state left in 1807 that still permitted the slave trade, the legislation didn't really stop the trade altogether. Estimates are that between ten thousand and twenty thousand blacks were still smuggled into the South every year, right up to the Civil War in 1861.

Even though the public Thomas Jefferson deplored and opposed the growth of slavery and its expansion into the territories, the private Jefferson seemed to be a concrete example of the South's dilemma. Like his staunchest opponents, Jefferson continued to hold slaves on his plantation at Monticello. During his presidency, Jefferson not only held slaves, but, according to reports, the third president bought as many as eight slaves while he occupied the White House between 1801 and 1808.

It appears that by the time he became president Jefferson had given up on the idea of doing anything about freeing the slaves. Although he had black acquaintances, like the scientist Benjamin Banneker, a free black mathematician, Jefferson subscribed to the prevailing theories of his time when it came to his ideas on the biological inferiority of the Negro race. Unlike the genuine abolitionists of the early years of the nineteenth century, who cared deeply about the condition of blacks, both slave and free, Jefferson was far more concerned with the evil effects of slavery on the life of white Virginians.

Indeed, there were many Americans in favor of ending slavery who were far ahead of Thomas Jefferson in both thought and action. Even in Virginia, enemies of slavery like Robert Pleasants and Warner Mifflin were more forceful in their quest for emancipation than was the third president of the United States, who lived off the labor of his slaves until his death in 1825.[7]

George Washington, the nation's first president and a Virginian with at least as much influence as Jefferson, wrote in 1786 that one of his great hopes was that a plan could someday be adopted "by which slavery may be abolished by slow, sure and imperceptible degrees." In the year Washington wrote those words, the few petitions to abolish slavery presented to the Virginia legislature were given little attention. Unlike Jefferson, however, Washington's conscience was so troubled by slavery that when he died he left a provision in his will freeing all of his slaves.

Although Jefferson freed a few slaves whom he called "faithful retainers" in his will, the slave system was so embedded in Virginia's way of life that few opponents had any real hope that it would die a natural death. Thomas Jefferson was so bound to the institution of slavery that, though he despised it, like most Virginians of his time he could never let it go.

Geographically, Virginia could be divided into four regions: The Tidewater area was a series of peninsulas that stretched out into Chesapeake Bay, affording access to the second region, the Piedmont, from a number of navigable riverways along the James, York, Rappahannock, and Potomac rivers. The other two regions of the state, the Shenandoah Valley and the mountain areas, were far from the ocean and therefore not at all suited to the plantation system that characterized the rest of Virginia. The whites who settled in Virginia to earn their living by planting mostly tobacco were largely dependent on the major river systems for transportation.

While the Tidewater region, close to the ocean, was best suited to commercial agriculture, it was the Piedmont region that expanded most rapidly. Nat Turner grew up in the early part of the nineteenth century, when the seat of Virginia state government was changed from Williamsburg to Richmond.

The major cash crop in Virginia's agricultural

economy was tobacco. By Jefferson's time, Virginia farmers were growing grains like wheat but always seemed to fall behind the productivity of their northern counterparts. Northern farmers often built large-scale mills to process their wheat into flour and had a flourishing export business. The Virginia planters put any profits back into land and slaves instead of into manufacturing or heavy industry.

At the base of Virginia's agricultural life was the institution of human slavery. As historian Robert McColley has written:

> The slave was fundamental in the large economic affairs of Virginia. One hardly can find an instance of productive activity in which Negro slaves were not engaged. Their wide use points much more to their adaptability than to the occasional view that the Negro slave was a lazy and indifferent worker, suited only to the simplest and most monotonous tasks.[8]

The slaves performed a wide variety of jobs. Some slaves were involved in growing staples, and others helped get the products to market. There were slaves with special skills on every larger plantation: slave coopers (barrelmakers) built barrels; slave blacksmiths forged the iron hoops that held the barrels together; slaves trained as teamsters labored to deliver the crops to the nearest large body of water for transport to market . Black boatmen could sail or pole the cargo downriver to warehouses, where it would be readied for transport to foreign markets or markets in other states. There were even black sailors who, though enslaved, made up the crews of the large sailing vessels engaged in the coastal and West Indies trade.

But by the nineteenth century, with slavery already abolished in England and under attack in the United States, the slaveowning master class in

Virginia increasingly tightened its control on the lives of slaves. The slaveowners wanted to limit severely the possibility of a slave rebellion. By 1822 the Virginia state legislature passed a very restrictive law to prevent mutiny. It prohibited a ship's crew from having more than one-third slave sailors. And, of course, slaves were not permitted to serve as captains of these ships.

The Western world's discomfort with slavery stemmed from social, religious, and political reasons. For one thing, the African slaves had become Christians, and it was clear to those in England and the United States who opposed slavery that the only thing that defined slavery in America was race. Many western Europeans and Americans were schooled in the Enlightenment (the philosophical movement of the eighteenth century that stressed the power of human reason), and influenced by the politics of the American and French revolutions. The idea of equality became the watchword of the era and slavery became incompatible with the progress of humankind.

More important for Virginians was the fact that belief in the inherent dignity of human beings had been fostered by a native son, one of the American Revolution's true heroes and the author of the Declaration of Independence, Thomas Jefferson. By Jefferson's time human slavery had become fundamentally incompatible with the direction in which the third president hoped to take his young nation.

Most historians agree that the life of a slave was far better in border states like Virginia, Maryland, and Tennessee than it was farther south, where crops and climate did much to change the nature of slavery. Perhaps the worst thing that could happen to a slave was to be "sold down river," a threat often used by masters with unruly or lazy slaves. It usually meant a hazardous journey into the deeper South to states like Mississippi, Alabama, Georgia, Louisiana, or Florida.

Most slaves knew that life there was harder, and conditions much more difficult. The states of the deep South had longer, hotter summers and larger plantations, where overseers generally controlled much of slave life. As John Hope Franklin has written, "It was in plantations where there were overseers that the greatest amount of cruelty and brutality existed."[9]

It must not be forgotten that the primary concern of the slaveowner was to get as much work as possible from his slaves. Small farmers holding only a few slaves generally got to know their slaves well and usually worked side by side with them in the fields and in the kitchens. However, on the larger plantations, usually consisting of between fifty and a hundred slaves, tasks were generally assigned to slaves according to skill. With this division of labor among slaves on large plantations, two distinct groups of slaves emerged: house servants and field hands.

House servants were the favored group and usually worked in the master's house, yards, and gardens. The house slave cooked the master's family meals, drove his fine carriages, and did anything required of a trusted personal servant. Favored house slaves often traveled with their masters and reaped other personal benefits in terms of better clothing, food, and even, up to a point, education.

The life of a field slave was much more difficult. Often, if a master couldn't afford house slaves, the field hands were required to perform double duty. The primary labor on the plantation was agricultural. Most field hands worked from dawn to dusk in the fields planting and harvesting crops like tobacco, cotton, rice, sugar, and indigo (a blue dye made from various plants). Except on rice plantations where slaves were given specific assignments every day, the gang system was used. As John Hope Franklin writes, "Literally, gangs of slaves were taken to the field and put to work under the supervision of the owner or overseer. The leader instructed them about when to begin work, when to eat, and when to quit. Slaves under this system were wholly without responsibility and had little opportunity to develop initiative.[10]

On Samuel Turner's small farm in Southampton County, Virginia, young Nat Turner was initiated into the work life of a field slave. Samuel Turner's farm did not have as many slaves or as much land as his father's place did. There was a handsome two-story, eight-room manor house where a bright young man like Nat Turner could easily have been utilized. But the stern Samuel Turner had little appreciation for the potential in his twelve-year-old slave. Despite Nat's obvious intelligence, like so many millions of other forgotten black faces in American history, young Nat was sent out with the other field hands to the grueling and backbreaking work in the cotton fields.

It must have been a shock to the young slave. He was separated at the age of twelve from his white playmates forever. And those same playmates would soon be ordering him about when they took their places as members of the master class in that strange hierarchy in the Old South perpetuated by the institution of slavery. No longer would young Nat Turner happily while away the hot Virginia summers wrestling, fishing, and swimming with the white children.

At the tender age of twelve, when most young boys are on the verge of the great adventure that is adolescence, Nat Turner learned the first important lesson of his brief life as his hopes for freedom in the future were dashed: that he was a slave and would remain a slave—another man's property until the day he died.

It is difficult to determine exactly how much the hard labor in Master Turner's cotton fields affected Nat Turner's later life. Clearly, the abrupt changes in the fun-filled routine of a bright young lad could not take place without some important consequences. It appeared, to those who knew him, that Nat adjusted to those seemingly endless days of forced labor, from sunup to sundown, as a bondsman. Sometimes, however, appearances can be deceptive.

No single sweeping observation about the daily life of American slaves in the Old South could ever be wholly accurate. Conditions and treatment differed from region to region, by the jobs assigned to the slaves, and by the size of the plantation. Most slaves did not feel compelled to work very hard unless they were forced to do so by their master or overseer. After all, the benefits would in most cases be the same no matter how hard the slaves worked. There were, however, always exceptions on a few innovative plantations where masters sometimes developed systems of rewards or bounties (premiums) in exchange for hard work by diligent slaves. As Kenneth M. Stampp notes, "How hard the slaves were worked depended upon the demands of individual masters and their ability to enforce them. These demands were always more or less tempered by the inclination of most slaves to minimize their unpaid toil."[11]

Thus, while southerners often complained about low productivity and laziness of their slaves, it seems clear that slaves had few incentives to work hard. Instead of being lazy, most slaves soon caught on to the fact that they did not have to work very hard if they could get away with it. As John Hope Franklin writes, "There was a great deal of complaining about the idleness and laziness of slaves, but such was inherent in a system of forced labor."[12]

Even George Washington was heard to complain that his slave carpenters were lazy and that none of his house slaves could be trusted. Slaves, for the most part, did as little as possible. This was one of the reasons the plantation owners and smaller farmers continually felt the need to increase their productivity by acquiring more slaves.

In Virginia, conditions under which the slaves worked and lived were far better than those in the deep South, even though the work schedules were somewhat similar. Like the slaves in Arkansas and Missouri, the Virginia slave would often get up as early as four-thirty in the morning and toil until sundown or beyond. All in all, it was a hard life even under the best of conditions. By its very nature, slavery was oppressive in both a physical and a psychological sense, and slaves did their best to adjust to the conditions of slave life in order to survive. As John W. Blassingame notes:

> Once they acquired the language of their master, the Africans learned that their labors, and therefore their lives, were of considerable value. As a result, they were assured of the bare minimum of food, shelter and clothing. Although provisions were often inadequate and led to many complaints from slaves, they survived.[13]

But not all slaves survived the cruelty inherent in slavery. In the more difficult climate of South Carolina, for example, the survival of a slave who labored in the rice swamps was said to be three years on average, as the hard conditions often led to sickness, disease, and early death. However, Virginia slave life was still very difficult even though, by Jefferson's and Nat Turner's time, the treatment of a Virginia slave had become milder and more humane than in colonial days.

One Virginia observer felt that the slaves were worked like draft animals, although he went on to say that they seemed content. Another Virginian felt that slaves were well treated only on the larger planta-tions. Recording his thoughts on the treatment of slaves on smaller farms in his diary, Isaac Weld, Jr., a traveler, wrote: "The lot of such as are unfortunate enough to fall into the hands of lower class white people, and of hard task-masters in the towns, is very different."[14]

Still, other observers felt that the slave master who owned only a few slaves and therefore worked closely with them usually provided more kindness and humanity than did the planters on the large plan-tations, who would tend to employ an overseer.

The diet of the slaves varied from plantation to plantation, but few slaves enjoyed luxury eating. Meat was considered a delicacy, and although some slaves were permitted to raise their own vegetables and livestock, for the most part slaves did not eat as well as their masters. Corn, wheat, bacon, molasses, and other grains were staples in the diet of most slaves. On holidays like Christmas, slaves were occa-sionally rewarded with whiskey and rum.

Clothing was often crude but adequate. Slaveowners would not allow their property to freeze to death in the winter, and the fact that records indi-cate that many slaves were skilled as shoemakers may mean that the slaves rarely had to worry about cold feet in chillier weather.

Housing was another story. The kind and quality of shelter available to the slaves varied, from crudely built dirt-floor huts with beds of straw to well-built and adequately furnished wooden cabins.

What made life hardest for the slaves in Virginia, as in every section of the South, were the laws that strictly controlled every aspect of their lives. Slaves could not freely travel, move about their various com-munities, or enjoy any of the freedoms other Americans took for granted in the early nineteenth century.

Even free blacks led circumscribed lives. Virginia had the largest population of free blacks in the United States: 30,269 by 1810. Virginia's slave population by that year was over 392,000. The primary responsibility for control of slaves rested with their masters. Slaves convicted of serious crimes were usually hanged after thirty days. Owners of slaves who were convicted and executed were generally reimbursed for the market value of the slave out of public funds.[15]

Slaves who broke the law were brought to trial. When convicted of minor offenses like stealing, punishment could often be brutal. The common punishment was thirty-nine lashes. But burning, maiming, and other cruel forms of punishment were not unknown in southern history. Kenneth M. Stampp documents many of these outrageous cruelties in his study *The Peculiar Institution*. Still, Stampp is careful to point out that there were laws to protect slaves. As one southern judge noted, "A slave is not in the condition of a horse.... He has mental capacities, and an immortal principle in his nature."

It was against the law for a master to kill or maim his slaves without a trial. Almost every southern legislature extended some legal protection and rights to the slaves. Masters could be fined for mistreating or failing to feed and clothe their slaves adequately. While early colonial slave codes provided only light or no penalties for killing a slave, by 1788, states like Virginia and North Carolina made the murdering of a slave comparable to the killing of a freeman. Eventually, all of the southern states adopted laws to protect the lives of slaves even if the penalties did not seem to be overly harsh in some cases. However, there are recorded instances where cruel masters were brought to trial and to justice for maiming or murdering their slaves.

Still, it must be remembered that the laws of the nineteenth-century South were not designed to protect the slaves. As one historian of slavery in Virginia wrote:

> The evidence of one credible white man was sufficient to convict a slave, though of course no Negro, slave or free, could be a witness against a white. Negro testimony was admissible only in cases where Negroes alone were concerned.... The only law which offered special protection to colored Virginians was that which made a capital offense either of the stealing of slaves or the kidnapping of free Negroes.[16]

This then was slavery in Virginia during the era of Thomas Jefferson and Nat Turner. Jefferson's opposition to slavery, no matter how profound in a philosophical sense, meant very little to the daily lives of the slaves. If slavery were to be effectively challenged in Virginia, or elsewhere, many enemies of slavery believed that the challenge would have to come from the slaves themselves and from their white allies— from those who hated slavery enough that they would be willing to kill or even die to end it. Perhaps no one understood this better than Jefferson himself. Writing to a friend in 1820, the aging ex-president reflected on the question of slavery in the new Louisiana territories. The Missouri Compromise of 1820 had enabled the new states of Missouri and Maine to be admitted to the Union as a slave state and free state respectively. But Jefferson worried about the future as the territories were settled and divided into free and slave states. He wrote: "this momentous question, like a fire-bell in the night, awakened and filled me with terror. I considered it at once as the knell of the Union. It is hushed, indeed, for the moment. But this is a reprieve only.... We have the wolf by the ears, and we can neither hold him, nor safely let him go."[17]

36

Jefferson, of course, could not have been aware that the fire-bell had already begun to toll in Southampton County, Virginia, where Nat Turner was growing into angry young adulthood. Indeed, Nat was to turn out to be the very wolf that Jefferson had in mind when he predicted that the issue of slavery would one day devour the beloved Union that he and the nation's founders in 1776 had so carefully constructed.

3

To Make the Master Stand in Fear: Slave Rebellions in the South

Brethren, arise, arise! Strike for your lives and liberties. Now is the day and the hour. Let every slave throughout the land do this and the days of slavery are numbered. Rather die freemen than live to be slaves.... Awake, Awake, no oppressed people have secured their liberty without resistance.

—Henry Highland Garnet,
black abolitionist

Until the early part of the nineteenth century, as Nat Turner came of age on the Turner plantation, white southerners, slaveowners and nonslaveowners alike, did not seem overly concerned about the possibility of violent rebellion among the slaves in their midst. Perhaps it was because slavery, by its very nature, was so overwhelming and restrictive that most southerners did not pay close attention to the possibility of any serious resistance. Then it was that slavery came under political and armed attack.

Many Americans began to change the way they viewed slavery and found it to be fundamentally incompatible with democracy. With the philosophy of the equality of all people that grew out of the American and French revolutions, groups began to form with the express purpose of abolishing slavery. As these individuals, called abolitionists, became better organized and more influential, opposing groups formed in the South.

More important, perhaps, were two major slave revolts that took place in the South before 1830: the Gabriel Plot of 1800 in Virginia and the more famous Vesey Conspiracy of 1822 in South Carolina. These two rebellions frightened the South, and discouraged any inclinations that might have existed to end slavery. Instead of moving to a time of free and open discussion on how best to do away with slavery, many southerners, even nonslaveholders, became more militant in their defense of slavery. With that increasing militance came increasing controls over the slave population and stepped-up vigilance against the possibility of slave rebellion.

Southerners had always used armed might and physical force as the main instruments to control their slaves. Most southern communities enjoyed the presence of large detachments of regular federal troops in addition to the well-organized state militias. And there was at least one armed white person, the master or overseer, on every farm and plantation in the South.

By the 1850s, when the well-known writer, landscape architect, and journalist Frederick Law Olmsted traveled throughout the slave states to report on the status of slavery, his journals were filled with observations that southerners kept weapons handy and that wherever he went he met armed southerners. Commenting on his meeting with an overseer in the deep South, Olmsted wrote: "He always carried a bowie knife, but not a pistol unless he anticipated some unusual act of insubordination. He always kept a pair of pistols ready loaded over the mantel-piece, however, in case they should be needed."[1]

By the 1850s, the white South clearly lived in constant fear of slave uprisings. How had this come about, and was the fear justified? More to the point, how important were the few slave uprisings? What was their impact on Nat Turner's time and even on Nat Turner himself?

Some historians have claimed that there was violent opposition and some form of resistance to slavery from the very beginning. In his book *American Negro Slave Revolts*, historian Herbert Aptheker lists at least 250 reported slave conspiracies and revolts. Aptheker wonders how many uprisings were quickly put down and thus were lost to history by going unreported. Undoubtedly, there must have been some. But many of the incidents cited by Aptheker were little more than slaves refusing to work, striking a master, or performing singular acts of mischief or insubordination.

However, it appears that too many students of slavery have repeatedly asked the wrong questions about black resistance to slavery. Like Aptheker, they want to know why so many slave rebellions met such limited success. However, the brutal truth of the matter is that there was precious little organized resistance to American slavery.

Unlike the well-organized slave revolts in Latin America, well-planned slave rebellions in the United States were few and far between. For example, in 1800 a large-scale slave uprising against France took place in Haiti. A major force of French troops was defeated. This so discouraged Napoleon in his adventures in empire building in the Americas that in 1803 he sold all of his North American holdings to the United States. The famous Louisiana Purchase almost doubled the size of the United States and was a major accomplishment of the Jefferson administration.[2]

For the most part, however, American slave revolts were poorly organized and haphazard. Thus, a far better question to ask is why there was so little organized resistance to slavery. Some scholars attribute it to the oppressive nature of American slavery. Slave life was total. It encompassed and controlled every aspect of the slave's daily life and everyday behavior. And further, like some totalitarian governments of the twentieth century, slavery took over the slave's very being and obliterated virtually every vestige of his or her spontaneity, creativity, and originality. American slavery destroyed much of that spirit of independence and spark of ambition that exists at one time or another in all human beings.

Some early scholars saw slavery as benign. Yale University's Ulrich B. Phillips, who grew up in Georgia, was among the first to write and teach about American slavery. Phillips, whose first book on slavery was published in 1918, had a distorted and romantic notion about the southern past and did his best to assure his readers that blacks were well off as slaves. He argued that cruelty was exceedingly rare and that slavery civilized blacks.

We now know that the Old South was hardly a placid section and that the slaves were hardly docile or happy. Underneath what seemed to be a relaxed and tranquil society there existed turmoil, tension, and the ever-present possibility that the slaves would one day rise up against their masters. By Nat Turner's time this very real fear had become an increasingly documented reality. Even Professor Phillips came to recognize this fact. He wrote:

A great number of southerners at all times held the firm belief that the negro population was so docile, so little cohesive, and in the main so friendly toward the whites and so contented that a disastrous insurrection by them would be

41

impossible. But on the whole there was much greater anxiety abroad in the land than historians have told of, and its influence in shaping southern policy was much greater than they have appreciated.[3]

The importance of the slave revolts in the Old South has nothing to do with how many of them occurred or the extent of their success. For one thing, the American slaves faced hopeless odds in that they were overwhelmingly outnumbered. For another, the slaves in most cases had the added burden of being without firearms since it was against most southern laws for slaves to own guns. The fact that rebellions or uprisings took place at all is a testament to the courage of the slaves who led them and to their strong belief that their cause was honorable and just. As Eugene D. Genovese has written,

A slave revolt anywhere in the Americas, at any time, had poor prospects and required organizers with extraordinary daring and resourcefulness. In the United States those prospects, minimal during the eighteenth century, declined toward zero during the nineteenth. The slaves of the Old South should not have to answer for their failure to mount more frequent and effective revolts; they should be honored for having tried at all under the most discouraging circumstances.[4]

Yet try they did. One of the largest known slave revolts in the United States took place in Louisiana in 1811, involving between three hundred and five hundred slaves. During the afternoon of January 9, 1811, the citizens of New Orleans were amazed to find hundreds of whites fleeing from the parishes of St. Charles and St. John the Baptist, which were about 35 miles (56 km) from the city. They had fled from an armed contingent of slaves led by Charles Deslondes, a free black from Santo Domingo. The uprising had begun at the plantation of a Major Andry, where, after killing his son and wounding Andry, the slaves seized several firearms and began going from plantation to plantation urging other slaves to join their cause. According to reports, they killed at least one other white man and burned a few neighboring plantations.

Eventually, Major Andry himself organized some planters and led a counterattack on the slaves. At around the same time, Louisiana's Governor William C. Claiborne called out four hundred of the state militia and, with sixty regular U.S. Army soldiers, left New Orleans to link up with some two hundred additional army regulars from Baton Rouge. The rebellious slaves were attacked the next morning and defeated. Sixty-six slaves were killed or executed on the spot. Other leaders of the rebellion were tried in New Orleans and sentenced to death by hanging or firing squad. In a grisly warning to other would-be slave rebels in the region, the heads of the executed slaves were "strung aloft at intervals from New Orleans to Andry's plantation." A few months later the state passed a law compensating the masters whose slaves were killed or executed. Eventually, $29,000 was paid out, and Governor Claiborne wrote in a final public statement on the subject: "I hope this dreadful Insurrection is at an end and I pray God we may never see another."[5]

The Louisiana slave uprising, however, did not capture the South's attention by heightening its ever-present fears of slave revolt and insurrection. In fact, only two uprisings before Nat Turner's rebellion were deemed important enough for historians to mention in most American history textbooks.

The first took place in 1800, the year of Nat Turner's birth, and was led by Gabriel Prosser, a twenty-four-year old slave. Prosser helped to organize a large-scale slave conspiracy that ultimately resulted in widespread fear and alarm throughout the slave South.

Gabriel was described as a "giant of six feet two inches [18.5 m]" and as "a fellow of courage and intellect above his rank in life." His master, Thomas H. Prosser of Henrico County, Virginia, was reported to have "behaved with great barbarity to his slaves."

Like many of the slave revolts that never really succeeded, the Gabriel plot is steeped in mystery. And since Gabriel Prosser did not help clear up the matter when he was captured, we have only the records of the white southerners to tell us what happened.

It seems clear that Gabriel's plot was formed by the spring of 1800. It was apparently so widespread that word of it had even reached Virginia's governor. In a letter to his good friend Thomas Jefferson, dated April 22, 1800, Governor James Monroe expressed his "fears of a negro insurrection." Whether or not Governor Monroe was writing about Gabriel Prosser is uncertain, but it is clear that, by August 9, Governor Monroe had received a serious warning about the possibility of a slave rebellion in or around Richmond. The warning came in a letter from Petersburg, a town close to Richmond, where it was said that the slaves were conspiring to revolt.

According to the reports Monroe received, every Sunday the slave Gabriel Prosser would visit Richmond with the intent of organizing the slaves. At the same time, he was studying the layout of the city. Gabriel also wanted to find out the location of guns and ammunition in Richmond. The slaves thought that their plans were going well. They had secretly fashioned crude swords and bayonets as well as five hundred bullets to be used in their rebellion. Gabriel's plan seemed to be to organize a large slave army that would fight its way into Richmond and take the city. Then, he apparently hoped, word would spread and

44

slaves would flee from their plantations to join his free slave army in Richmond.

However, the authorities received final confirmation about Gabriel's rebellion on August 30, when two slaves, Tom and Pharaoh, told their master, Mosby Sheppard, of the plot. Sheppard quickly informed Governor Monroe. Monroe immediately placed cannons around the capitol, called up 650 troops and sent warnings about the eventuality of a slave revolt in Richmond to every militia commander in the state.

That very night, between a thousand and eleven hundred slaves gathered on the outskirts of Richmond. Some were on horseback, and most were armed with clubs, farm implements, and homemade bayonets. There were even a few who had firearms. Gabriel's army of slaves was well organized, and there was a plan. The slaves were to form three columns, each under the direction of a slave officer, and the army would then march on Richmond. One column would seize the penitentiary, which was then serving as the state's arsenal. With enough guns and ammunition, the slave leaders reasoned that they could take and hold the city. The second column was to seize the powder magazine in another part of the city; and the third was supposed to begin killing and slaughtering anyone who attempted to stop them, with the idea of terrorizing the city and the citizenry into submission.

It is highly unlikely that the slave army would have prevailed against the better-armed army regulars sent out by Governor Monroe. Eventually, the whites would have simply overwhelmed the slaves in terms of sheer numbers. But no real fighting ever took place. Fate worked against the slaves in the form of bad weather. As the slaves were gathering, just about sunset, a terrible storm hit the Richmond area. If they were going to invade Richmond, the slave army would first have to cross a wide swamp. But because

45

of the heavy rains from the storm, the bridge across the swamp was rendered impassable, and the dismayed slave army dispersed in confusion.

Over the next few days the machinery of repression of an agitated slave state sprang into action. Dozens of blacks were hunted down and arrested by state authorities. Gabriel Prosser himself escaped by ship to Norfolk, Virginia. But on September 25, he was recognized by two blacks in the city; he was betrayed, captured, and returned to Richmond in chains for trial.

Gabriel was sentenced to be hanged immediately, but his execution was postponed until October 7 in the hope that he would divulge to the authorities more about the conspiracy and perhaps even name others involved in the plot. Governor Monroe himself, who eventually became the fifth president of the United States, traveled to Richmond to interview Prosser. But Prosser seemed determined to take the secrets of his rebellion to his grave. As Governor Monroe reported: "From what he said to me, he seemed to have made up his mind to die, and to have resolved to say but little on the subject of the conspiracy."

On October 7, 1800, Gabriel Prosser and fifteen other slave rebels were hanged. Twenty-one slaves had been executed before October 7, and four more were scheduled to die for their part in the conspiracy. The courage of the condemned slaves was secretly admired by at least one Richmond citizen, who wrote: "Of those who have been executed, no one has betrayed his cause. They have uniformly met death with fortitude." It cannot be doubted that the slaves who conspired with Gabriel believed their cause to be just. They saw themselves as men no different from the heroes of the American Revolution. An Englishman visiting Virginia in 1804 passed by the field where some of the slaves had been executed and spoke with a lawyer who had apparently recorded some of the last thoughts of one of the slave rebels. The slave, asked to defend himself and his action, told the court what he felt about participating in Gabriel Prosser's aborted rebellion. According to the Englishman, the condemned slave responded:

I have nothing more to offer than what General Washington would have had to offer, had he been taken by the British and put to trial by them. I have adventured my life in endeavouring to obtain the liberty of my countrymen, and am a willing sacrifice to their cause: and I beg, as a favour, that I may be immediately led to execution. I know that you have pre-determined to shed my blood, why then all this mockery of a trial?

Much of the South shuddered in fear during the aftermath of Gabriel Prosser's conspiracy. As word of the rebellion spread, the slaveowners knew that their slaves would be discussing the events that took place in and around Richmond. Some supporters of slavery wanted the rebellion treated as a vicious and heinous crime, with the most drastic penalties available. Others wanted the slaves to know that they would be rewarded if they remained loyal to their masters. The two slaves who betrayed Prosser, Tom and Pharaoh, were rewarded. Governor Monroe ordered the state to pay their master $500 to purchase their freedom.

Even the governor, however, couldn't help but admire the courage of the slave rebels. When Monroe asked Thomas Jefferson for advice about carrying out the executions of the slave leaders, Jefferson replied, "The other states & the world at large will forever condemn us if we indulge a principle of revenge, or go one step beyond absolute necessity. They cannot lose sight of the rights of the two parties, & the object of the unsuccessful one." As a result, instead of being exe-

47

cuted, ten of the condemned slave leaders were allowed to live, although they were banished from Virginia forever and sold to another section of the South.[6]

Still, the Gabriel uprising resulted in a tightening of controls over the slaves of Virginia and in other parts of the South. In Richmond a number of laws were introduced to rein in the limited freedom the slaves enjoyed, and after another scare of rebellion in 1802, there was even talk of banishing newly freed slaves from the state altogether. The Virginia legislature became so touchy about the issue that when Jefferson became president they requested that he negotiate with an African nation so that any slave suspected of conspiracy to rebel could easily be deported from the state.[7]

If the Gabriel conspiracy of 1800 unsettled the Virginians, another uprising—the alleged plot by Denmark Vesey in Charleston, South Carolina—reverberated throughout the entire South. In many ways it helped set the stage for Nat Turner's bloody entrance into the pages of American history less than a decade later.

Many of the facts of the Vesey conspiracy are still shrouded in mystery and legend. One reason for this is that the Charleston newspapers imposed what today would be called total censorship of the facts surrounding the uprising. The newspapers reported little of what actually happened and were content to inform their readers about the sentences and executions of the conspirators. Thus, the record is sparse. We are forced to rely on little more than the "official" record published by the city of Charleston some months after the events took place.

Denmark Vesey was once a slave who was said to have been born in Africa. A skilled seaman who worked on slave traders, Vessey was also said to be well traveled and able to speak several languages, in addition to knowing how to read and write. By 1800,

Vesey had saved enough money to purchase his freedom. He settled near Charleston, where he labored as an artisan.

Like other slave leaders, Denmark Vesey appeared to be a deeply religious man. He would often justify his objections to slavery by reading a passage from the Bible about "how the children of Israel were delivered out of Egypt from bondage." Vesey would often become angry if he saw a black friend acting subserviently to a white person. He would constantly remind his followers that all people were born equal and "that he would never cringe to the whites, nor ought any who had the feelings of a man."[8]

Still, exactly what Vesey was doing in that hot summer of 1822 is not clear. As historian Richard C. Wade has written,

> It was generally believed at the time that the blacks had hatched a plot on the grandest scale to overthrow white rule by force, butcher masters and mistresses, sack the city, and then escape into the Caribbean. The numbers involved presumably ran into thousands, and only a last minute betrayal scotched its successful execution.[9]

As in the Gabriel Prosser rebellion, it was slaves who passed the word to whites about the prospect of armed resistance to slavery in Charleston. On May 25, 1822, two slaves met casually on the fish wharf of Charleston harbor. The slaves, William Paul and Devany Prioleau, were chatting about the ships in the harbor when Paul asked Prioleau if he had heard the rumor that "something serious is about to take place." Then, to the astonished Prioleau, William Paul was even more to the point: "many of us are determined," he said, "to right ourselves" and "shake off our bondage." Devany Prioleau had heard enough. He broke off the conversation and quickly hurried off.

After a few days, Prioleau confided what he had heard to another friend, a free black by the name of George Pencil. Pencil told him to tell his owner, and that is exactly what he did. On May 30, Devany Prioleau informed his mistress about what he had heard in Charleston harbor.[10]

Later, when other slave conspirators were questioned, they told the court that they had been careful never to speak to any other blacks about what they were doing for fear of betrayal. Indeed, as one of the slave conspirators, Peter Poyas, had warned, "Take care and don't mention it to those waiting men who receive presents of old coats, etc., from their masters, or they'll betray us."[11]

By five o'clock that afternoon, after Mrs. Prioleau had alerted the city authorities, the mayor called the city council into session, and the police were sent out to pick up both Prioleau and William Paul. Paul was kept in solitary confinement for a week before he finally gave the police two names: Mingo Harth and Peter Poyas. The two men were picked up but apparently were able to convince the police that they were innocent and knew nothing of a plot to produce a slave rebellion in the city.

The police were frustrated. Nothing could be proved. Still, the mayor decided to step up and strengthen the armed patrols around the city. The authorities watched and waited.

According to the "Official Report," Vesey had picked the second Sunday in July for his uprising. Since Sunday was a day off for most slaves, many would be allowed to enter the city, and in July many whites, to escape the heat of the city, were away. But the betrayal forced him to move the date ahead by almost a month, to June 16. Vesey's problem, common in an era when there were no telephones or fax machines, was that he had great difficulty communicating the fact that his conspiracy had been betrayed and that he was moving up the date of the rebellion. Many of his slave allies were hard to reach on the outlying plantations that could be as far away from Charleston as 80 miles (129 km).

Unfortunately for the slaves, the authorities got the break they waited for on June 14, when another slave came forward and told essentially the same story as William Paul. Convinced that something indeed was going on, the police appeared in and around the city in force. Even though nothing happened on June 16, on June 18 ten slaves were arrested. On June 21, Denmark Vesey was arrested, and by July 2, six slaves had been executed for a plot that never even took place.[12]

The conspirators were determined to die taking the secret of the Vesey plot to their graves. As one of them, Peter Poyas, said, "Die silent, as you shall see me do." Thus, it is difficult to piece together just what the plot entailed and how many blacks were involved. Some witnesses offered up the fantastic figures of from 6,600 to 9,000 slaves ready to simultaneously attack Charleston in a militarily coordinated six-prong assault. Those numbers appear to be inflated. Still, it appears that the Vesey conspiracy was extensive and did involve the secret gathering of arms by large numbers of slaves in the area.[13]

One historian even says that the slaves were divided up by African tribal affiliation with "the Angolas, the Eboes and the Carolina-born...separately organized under appropriate commanders." Whatever the reality and extent of the Vesey rebellion, there was no question that it was betrayed and that it was nipped in the bud. The blacks were tried under court rules that said no slave could be convicted unless represented by the presence of his master or an attorney; that every slave could testify in his own defense; and that no one would be executed on the testimony of a single witness.

When all was said and done, 130 blacks were arrested, including 9 free blacks. Of that number, twenty-five were discharged by a committee and twenty-seven were discharged by the court. Nine others were acquitted with recommendations by their masters that they be transported from the area. Of the blacks convicted, thirty-four were deported, and thirty-five were hanged. In addition, four white men were indicted for complicity in the plot and sentenced to terms in prison ranging from three to twelve months. Devany Prioleau was given his freedom and an annual pension of $50, which was raised in 1857 to $250. The free black, George Pencil, was awarded $1,000 by the state of South Carolina.[14]

Denmark Vesey went to the gallows refusing to confirm the fact that he had organized a vast conspiracy. But in the next series of trials, three of the slaves who had been sentenced to death implicated many other blacks when they were promised leniency. Whether or not they did this to save their lives is impossible to tell.[15]

As the "Official Report" of the Vesey plot finally stated,

Enough has been disclosed to satisfy every reasonable mind, that considerable numbers were involved.... It extended to the North of Charleston many miles towards Santee, and unquestionably into St. John's Parish; to the South to James' and John's Islands; and to the West beyond Bacon's Bridge over Ashley River.[16]

Once again, as news of the Vesey conspiracy spread throughout the South, whites began to wonder about the supposedly contented blacks who lived and worked among them. Charleston's large black community had seemed tranquil enough on the surface. The Charleston blacks were more literate than the slaves in the rural sections of South Carolina and were permitted to engage in skilled labor. After all, Denmark Vesey was a free man and a skilled carpenter. Why would a man throw away his livelihood along with his life to organize and lead a hopeless rebellion that was doomed to failure from the very start? It was a question that would trouble the sleep of many a white southerner in the difficult years ahead. As slave controls proliferated with increased patrolling and surveillance throughout many regions of the South, white southerners watched and waited uneasily for the next shoe to drop. As one group of Charleston citizens warned shortly after the Vesey conspiracy, "We should always act as if we had an enemy in the very bosom of the state."[17]

Although some historians still believe today that "the 'plot' was probably never more than loose talk by aggrieved and embittered men," the Vesey conspiracy stirred up the proslavery and antislavery forces throughout the nation. Defenders of slavery argued that the conspiracy showed the clear need for further controls on slaves and on free Negroes. Those who attacked slavery expanded their case by noting that even free blacks or well-treated slaves would never accept the cruelty and inequality inherent in the institution of slavery. All people, they told anyone who would listen to their argument, yearn to be free and would eventually give up everything, including their lives, to prove it.[18]

In Southampton County, Virginia, the slave called Nat Turner was waiting to step forward into the pages of American history to advance that argument one violent and bloody step further.

4

The Rebellion Takes Root in Southampton County, Virginia

*Remember Americans, that we must and shall be free
and enlightened as you are, will you wait until we
shall, under God, obtain our liberty by the crushing
arm of power? Will it not be dreadful for you?*

—David Walker,
from his 1829 *Appeal*

With the debate over slavery accelerating in the North
and South in the aftermath of the Vesey plot, both sides
began to harden their positions on the question. It is
clear, however, that the South was on the defensive as
the abolitionists organized, held public meetings, and
began a concerted assault on slavery that did not end
until the last shot of the Civil War was fired in 1865.

Southerners mounted a defense of slavery that
reached as far back as the Greeks and Aristotle's ideas
about order and function in society. They examined
the Bible to show that slavery was part of the moral
and natural order, and they even postulated what

became known as the "King Cotton" theory, which demonstrated that the necessities of world trade relied on slavery's economic foundation. Mostly, however, the defenders of slavery did their best to show that the Negro was an inferior race by using the theories of science that prevailed in that era.

Since such distorted racial theories were not discredited until well into the twentieth century, this argument was often utilized with savage ferocity. Even many well-meaning abolitionists accepted the idea that blacks were racially inferior to whites.

What was especially troubling to the supporters of slavery in the South was the widespread distribution of speeches and pamphlets that not only attacked slavery, but also urged blacks and their allies to rise up against "the peculiar institution" in any way possible. As the Prosser and Vesey uprisings had proved, the South was afraid that one day their slaves would unite in rebellion and demand a terrible retribution for over two centuries of oppression and degradation. This shift in southern thought, from apology for slavery to aggressive defense of it, came directly on the heels of the Vesey conspiracy. As one historian has noted, "the most pervading legacy of the trauma Denmark Vesey wrought was a compulsion to check abolitionist propaganda and to stop congressional slavery debates."[1]

By the late 1820s, two strands of abolitionist thought stood out in the struggle against slavery. There were those who called for violence in the crusade against slavery. These people argued that slavery was such an overriding evil that any means necessary, including violent rebellion, could be used to stop it.

The other school of thought was best represented by people like William Lloyd Garrison of Massachusetts, who became the most articulate spokesman for nonviolence even though he was militantly opposed to every aspect of slavery. Like many others who were deeply troubled by slavery, Garrison had once been a supporter of the idea of colonization—deporting slaves back to Africa or setting up an island for blacks somewhere in the Caribbean.

By 1830, Garrison had abandoned the idea of colonization, breaking ties with Henry Clay, a Kentucky congressman who, as the most prominent member of the Colonization Society, hoped to one day become president of the United States. Garrison made it known that he looked forward to the day when Clay became president, but he rejected Clay's notion that whites were superior to Native Americans or any other race, saying, "I deny the postulate, that God has made, by an irreversible decree, or any inherent qualities, one portion of the human race superior to another." Garrison didn't feel that anyone associated with slavery could argue the issue fairly or objectively. In 1830 he wrote:

It is morally impossible, I am convinced, for a slaveholder to reason correctly on the subject of slavery. His mind is warped by a thousand prejudices, and a thick cloud rests upon his mental vision. He was really taught to believe, that a certain class of beings was born for servitude, whom it is lawful to enthral, and over whom he is authorized—not merely by the law of his native state, but by Jehovah himself—to hold unlimited dominion.[2]

In January 1831, Garrison distributed the first issue of his antislavery publication *The Liberator*, which demanded an immediate end to slavery in the United States. Writing from Boston, Garrison challenged slavery more dramatically than anyone in the past had, saying, "I will be as harsh as truth, and as uncompromising as justice. On this subject, I do not wish to think, to speak, or write, with moderation.... I am in earnest—I will not equivocate—I will not excuse—I will not retreat a single inch—AND I WILL BE HEARD."[3]

Garrison began to travel and speak in a dozen northern cities, where he addressed largely black audiences in a standard speech saying, "I never rise to address a colored audience, without feeling ashamed of my own color, ashamed of being identified with a race of men who have done you so much injustice." Garrison immediately began to attract large-scale support from free blacks in the larger cities. James Forten, a successful black Philadelphian who had fought in the American Revolution, sent Garrison money for twenty-seven subscriptions to *The Liberator*, noting, "I am extremely happy to hear that you are establishing a Paper in Boston. I hope your efforts may not be in vain; and that the 'Liberator' be the means of exposing more and more the odious system of Slavery, and of raising up friends to the oppressed and degraded People of Colour throughout the Union."[4]

Southerners were so alarmed by the publication of Garrison's *Liberator* that he was vilified in the press. Georgia even put a $500 price on his head, urging his capture and his transportation to the state. Governor John Floyd of Virginia believed that Garrison's intention was "inciting the slaves and free negroes in this and the other States to rebellion and to murder the men, women and children of those states." Governor Floyd insisted that publication of *The Liberator* be halted. Many communities in the South tried to prevent its distribution and worried that it would fall into the hands of their slaves.

Some southern historians believe that the South was unduly alarmed because Garrison never had more than three thousand subscribers, and his views were not only criticized in the North but also largely ignored by newspapers and other periodicals. By 1835 opposition to Garrison was so intense that he was seized by an angry mob of Boston businessmen and paraded through the streets of the city before being rescued by the police and taken to jail for his own safety.

Southerners who, in the past, had been moderate in their defense of slavery began to worry that their entire section of the nation was being isolated by the abolitionist's unrelenting assault.

In 1837, Senator John C. Calhoun of South Carolina, who had served as vice-president under President Andrew Jackson until resigning over the question of state's rights, asserted that "if we do not defend ourselves none will defend us; if we yield we will be more and more pressed as we recede; and if we submit we will be trampled underfoot."[5]

What caused people like Calhoun, who loved the Union and loved the South, to become increasingly defensive when it came to slavery? Everything points to the widespread fear that gripped the hearts of all southerners about the possibility of slave rebellion.

If any publication that circulated throughout the country helped to contribute to that fear, it was the appearance in 1829 of a pamphlet that advocated the use of violence to overthrow slavery. Published by David Walker, a free black in Boston, it was titled *Walker's Appeal in Four Articles Together with a Preamble to the Coloured Citizens of the World But in Particular and very Expressly to those of the United States of America.* Walker scorned slaveholding Christians of the South and wrote "that we (coloured people of these United States) are the most degraded, wretched, and abject set of beings that ever lived since the world began." In no uncertain terms and in clear language Walker urged that the slaves of the South rise up and cut their tormentor's throats.[6]

When *Walker's Appeal* reached the hands of the

white South, the reaction was immediate. Governors of states like Virginia, Georgia, and North Carolina called their legislatures into secret session in order to determine methods by which the *Appeal* could be kept out of the South and out of the hands of the slaves. For the first time, southerners seemed intent on drastically regulating freedom of speech and of the press.

No matter what precautions they took, however, the white South could not keep Walker's incendiary pamphlet from crossing their borders. In 1830, Walker was found beaten to death near his clothing shop in the North End section of Boston. But Walker's unsolved murder hardly silenced the fiery words of his *Appeal*.

There is no hard evidence to suggest that Walker's *Appeal* ever got into the hands of Nat Turner, who, by the year of its publication, had become well known in Southampton County, Virginia, as a mystical slave-preacher. Of course, there is no evidence to suggest that Turner didn't read it. Certainly, the timing of the *Appeal*'s publication is interesting in light of the events that were to transpire in and around Southampton County by the end of the summer of 1831. At the very least, Nat Turner knew about Denmark Vesey's plot and other slave uprisings. He also knew that other Virginia communities had been upset by the threat of slave rebellions. It was a time of great unrest in the South.[7]

Things had changed for the worse in Nat Turner's life. Life had been hard on the Turner farm, and Nat hadn't been a model slave. Because of a national depression in 1819 the cotton market had suffered a severe downswing. To get more work from his slaves, Samuel Turner hired an overseer to manage his farm. This may have prompted Nat to become a runaway and to live as a fugitive in 1821.[8]

The overseer may have beaten Nat because, as Nat said, "I was placed under an overseer, from whom I ran away." Nat remained in hiding in the nearby woods for thirty days. To the "astonishment of the negroes on the

59

plantation," who thought that he had escaped as his father had done, Nat returned of his own free will. Many of the slaves who knew him well were bewildered. As Turner recalled, "the negroes found fault, and murmured against me, saying that if they had my sense they would not serve any master in the world."

Why did Nat come back to a life of oppression under slavery? He was convinced that his mission in life forced him to return to the dreary toil of a field slave. Nat said, "the reason of my return was, that the Spirit appeared to me and said I had my wishes directed to the things of this world, and not to the Kingdom of Heaven, and that I should return to the service of my earthly master." Nat then quoted the passage from the Bible that many white slaveowners used in defending slavery: "For he who knoweth his Master's will, and doeth it not, shall be beaten with many stripes, and thus have I chastened you."[9]

A possible reason that Nat Turner returned to the sure punishment that awaited him on Samuel Turner's plantation was that he wanted to establish trust among his fellow slaves so that he would be free to organize among them as a leader in the future.

Shortly after his return Nat had a vision. He saw, he tells us,

---

White spirits and black spirits engaged in battle, and the sun was darkened—the thunder rolled in the Heavens, and blood flowed in the streams—and I heard a voice saying, "Such is your luck, such you are called to see, and let it come rough or smooth, you must surely bare [sic] it."[10]

It was also around this time that Nat Turner fell in love and was married. This may be another reason

Nat came back to a life of slavery. There was a female slave called Cherry on the Turner farm. No record exists of their courtship, but it seems clear that Nat Turner was a family man with a wife and children.

In 1822 tragedy struck Nat's family. His master, Samuel Turner, died, and the worst fears of every slave's life came to be realized on the Turner farm. With the price of cotton still low, Elizabeth Turner, Samuel Turner's widow, decided to sell her slaves at auction. There were virtually no restrictions on the rights of slaveowners to sell their slaves to anyone they chose. Slave families had no rights under the law and could be broken up whenever a master needed ready cash or chose to punish a recalcitrant slave. The anguish of slave families, shattered over two centuries of forced breakup, hardly mattered. This rupture of black family units was among the most sinister and evil aspects of slavery. Somehow, the structure of the black family survived. Slavery did not cause it to disintegrate altogether.

And so the Turner farm was broken up. Elizabeth Turner kept three slaves for domestic work, one of whom was Nat's mother. The other twenty slaves, including Nat and his new wife, were sold. Thus, Nat Turner experienced firsthand the most inhumane and brutal aspect of the life of a slave: the breakup of his beloved family. Nat Turner was sold to a new master named Thomas Moore, and his wife and children were sold to Giles Reese, a poorer farmer who rented a rundown place not far from the Moore farm.

If Nat's life on the Turner farm had been hard, his life on the Moore plantation was a living nightmare. Separated from his family and working for an ambitious master who had only three field slaves to farm more than 700 acres (200 hectares) of land, Nat Turner's days seemed endless. As one historian describes his workload,

Nat built the morning fires, hauled water, fed the cows, slopped the hogs, chopped wood, raised fences, repaired fences, cleared new fields, spread manure, and grew and gathered hay for the stock. In the spring, he struggled through the damp fields behind a mule-drawn plow. Most of the summer he chopped and cut and hoed in the corn and cotton patches, battling weeds, weevils, and the weather itself. Then he had to harvest the crops before winter set in, wrestling with gunnysacks of cotton, corn, and apples which Moore loaded in his wagon and took off to sell in Jerusalem on market Saturdays.[11]

We do not know much about Nat Turner's innermost thoughts during these trying years. He recalls that he kept to himself and did not have much to do with his fellow slaves. As Turner told Thomas R. Gray, after 1825, "I sought more than ever to obtain true holiness before the great day of judgment should appear, and then I began to receive true knowledge of faith." When Turner spoke of a "great day of judgment," there is little doubt that he meant to lead a revolution among the slaves.

Nat would go off into the woods or spend his free Sundays alone in his cabin, where he would read and reread passages from his Bible. The other slaves gradually accepted Nat as a visionary and a mystic. The vision Nat waited for finally came one day as he was working in a field. Nat discovered, he says, drops of blood on the corn "as though it were dew from heaven." As he walked in the woods, he found leaves with hieroglyphics (ancient Egyptian characters) and "numbers, with the forms of men in different attitudes, portrayed in blood, and representing the figures I had seen before in the heavens."

Nat was convinced that he had talked to God:

And now the Holy Ghost revealed itself to me,
and made plain the miracles it had shown me—
For as the blood of Christ had been shed on this
earth, and had ascended to heaven for the salva-
tion of sinners, and was now returning to earth
again in the form of dew—and as the leaves on
the trees bore the impression of the figures I had
seen in the heavens, it was plain to me that the
Saviour was about to lay down the yoke he had
borne for the sins of men, and the great day of
judgment was at hand.[12]

Soon Nat was preaching to the slaves. He became,
according to one observer, "the most eminent slave
preacher in his neighborhood." Nor did he attempt to
hide his visions and revelations from the whites who
lived nearby. He apparently told a white man by the
name of Etheldred T. Brantley about the visions, and
Turner remembered that "it had a wonderful effect—
and he ceased from his wickedness." Eventually,
Brantley was baptized by the young slave preacher.
This was shocking because whites and blacks were as
separate in their Christianity as they were in every
other aspect of their lives. It must have been quite a
sight when Turner took a white man to Pearson's Mill
Pond, northwest of Flat Swamp, for baptism in front
of a crowd of blacks and jeering whites.

Most likely, the whites who heard about Turner's
visions thought him a harmless crackpot. He worked
hard for Thomas and Sally Moore, so they didn't
seem to care very much if he preached to the slaves
on his free Sundays. Other whites apparently felt as
the Moores did. If Nat Turner's preaching kept their
slaves happy and working hard, then what bad could

come from that? By 1826, Nat Turner was looked upon with respect by the slaves on many of the surrounding farms and plantations. Although Nat wasn't considered a regularly ordained minister of the faith or even properly enrolled in any church, he was seen as a religious leader and was permitted to preach to the slaves at their Sabbath get-togethers.

On Sundays, Nat was free to travel about from farm to farm. He was even permitted to visit with his wife and children on the nearby Reese farm. That he could come and go so freely in a time when southern slaveowners were increasingly fearful of giving their slaves too much freedom shows that the whites must have trusted him implicitly. As a result, Nat soon came to know the region with all its woods, swamps, and back-country roads better than any slave in the county. And unlike most other blacks in Southampton County, he came to know many of the whites as well as he knew their slaves.[13]

The years passed as Nat Turner waited for another divine vision, for some direction. It did not matter that he had become an admired and respected preacher in the slave quarters every Sunday. For Nat Turner, Sunday was only one day out of seven. The rest of his week was spent as a slave.

On the surface—to the whites with whom he came in contact—Nat seemed to be the perfect slave. He was the picture of what southern whites expected in their slaves. Nat was polite and friendly; he worked hard for long hours, and aside from his bizarre claims about mystical and prophetic visions of God in the woods and fields, he made himself a trusted and valuable asset on the Moore farm.

However, underneath this facade of contentment, Nat's rage at his condition burned and festered like a concealed wound. He was like a time bomb ticking away in his master's cotton patches. All he needed

Benjamin Turner, and other nineteenth-century Virginia slaveholders, lived in comfortable two-story plantation houses.

A nineteenth-century drawing shows the crowded slave deck of a trade ship like those that were used to carry millions of people from Africa across the Middle Passage into slavery.

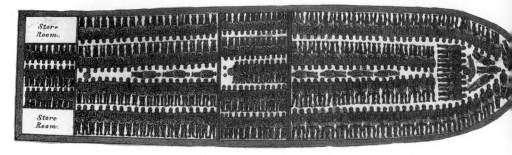

The slaves were "packed tight in the most inhuman way unable to breathe," as a physician observed and as this old lithograph of the plan of a slave ship shows.

Beginning in the seventeenth century, the slave trade provided labor for Virginia's sugar, tobacco, and cotton plantations.

Thomas Jefferson—here portrayed by the noted
eighteenth-century painter, Rembrandt Peale—
deplored the spread of slavery, yet was a
slaveholder himself and, as president,
was unable to end it.

In an old print, slaves who worked in their
master's house were depicted as
trusted personal servants.

Field hands, here cutting sugarcane,
worked through long days
of hard labor.

Slaves' homes varied from one plantation to another. Here a nineteenth-century artist shows the interior of a slave shanty near Petersburg, Virginia.

An illustration from nineteenth-century antislavery
literature dramatically presents the oppressive and
viciously destructive nature of slavery.

EVIDENCE

AGAINST THE VIEWS

OF THE

ABOLITIONISTS,

CONSISTING OF

PHYSICAL AND MORAL

PROOFS,

OF THE NATURAL INFERIORITY

OF THE

NEGROES.

BY RICHARD H. COLFAX.

NEW-YORK.

JAMES T. M. BLEAKLEY, PUBLISHER, 240

1833.

Defenders of slavery published impassioned arguments—sometimes claiming scientific evidence—to justify their position.

The writer and reformer, William Lloyd Garrison, was the publisher of a famous antislavery journal, *The Liberator*.

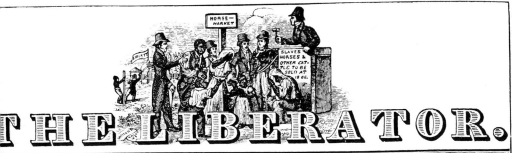

T H E L I B E R A T O R.

. I.]   WILLIAM LLOYD GARRISON AND ISAAC KNAPP, PUBLISHERS.   [NO. 22.

TON, MASSACHUSETTS.]   OUR COUNTRY IS THE WORLD—OUR COUNTRYMEN ARE MANKIND.   [SATURDAY, MAY 28, 1831.

In Nat Turner's Virginia, the death of a master could lead to a slave being sold at auction, and at the same time losing both family and home.

In a nineteenth-century engraving,
Nat Turner and his confederates are
seen planning their rebellion.

(Above) A nineteenth-century artist shows the moment when Nat Turner was discovered, after he had spent weeks hiding in a cave and among the stacks of wheat on Nathaniel Francis's farm.

(Below) Angry, frightened southerners burned the tracts and newspapers of the militant northern abolitionists they blamed for Nat Turner's violent rebellion.

Among the legislation that cruelly limited the lives of blacks were fugitive slave laws that stated that a person suspected of being a runaway could be seized and arrested.

(Left) A nineteenth-century artist's drawing depicts
the factors that led to the sectional split
between the North and South—slavery and the
plantation crops of cotton and sugarcane.

(Above) Nat Turner's rebellion generated anxiety
and heated debates over slavery in the Virginia
legislature, but the oppressive system continued
for slaves in the field.

In 1831 an illustrated account of Nat Turner's
rebellion was published, with the title page
pictured above, and the pictures shown here,
with this accompanying narrative: "The scenes
which the above Plate is designed to represent
—Fig. 1. a Mother intreating for the lives of her
children.—2. Mr. Travis cruelly murdered by his
own slaves.—3. Mr. Barrow, who bravely defended
himself until his wife escaped.—4. A company
of mounted dragoons in pursuit of the Blacks."

was someone or something to light the fuse. On May 12, 1828, Turner said:

I heard a loud noise in the heavens, and the Spirit instantly appeared to me and said the Serpent was loosened, and Christ had laid down the yoke he had borne for the sins of men, and that I should take it on and fight against the Serpent, for the time was fast approaching when the first should be last and the last should be first.

The fuse was now lit. Nat now knew what he had to do. The appearance of the sign meant, he said, that "I should arise and prepare myself, and slay my enemies with their own weapons."[14]

Nat didn't keep his feelings entirely to himself. When he told his master that slavery was wrong and that one day their freedom would come, Thomas Moore gave Nat a nasty beating.

Once again events intervened. Nat's master died before the end of 1828. Nat and the other slaves, now five in number, became the legal property of his master's nine-year-old son, Putnam Moore. Within a year the widow Moore married a local wheelwright, Joseph Travis. When Travis moved to the Moore farm, he assumed control of the slaves until his stepson, young Putnam, came of legal age.

Nat apparently got along well with his new master. He tells us that Travis was "a kind master, and placed the greatest confidence in me; in fact, I had no cause to complain of his treatment to me."[15]

Nat was permitted to keep his last name, which in the nineteenth-century slave South was somewhat unusual. Slaves usually assumed the last name of their current masters. This is an indication that his new master liked the mystical young preacher.

Some scholars have asserted that Nat then became a house slave and that, because his mistress liked him so much, the oppressive burden of working the fields and cotton patches was lifted from Nat's life when Sally Moore married Joseph Travis. There is, however, no evidence to indicate that Nat Turner ever became a house slave. There is no doubt that his master and mistress liked and trusted him. But this affection did not do anything to change his condition of servitude, and his work life continued as before. Of this period in his life, Turner tells us that he waited for another sign.

In February 1831, there was an eclipse of the sun. Taking the eclipse as visible proof of the much-awaited sign, Nat began to organize. He says, "I communicated the great work laid out for me to do, to four in whom I had the greatest confidence." These four slaves, Hark Travis, Nelson Williams, Sam Francis, and Henry (last name and owner unknown) became Nat's most trusted lieutenants. The five slaves met many times. Each time they formulated plans for a rebellion. And each time the plans were rejected. Nat wanted to begin what he called "the work of death" on the Fourth of July. Obviously, he had an acute sense of American history. But he became ill, and with so many schemes mulling around in his mind, the July 4 date came and passed.

On August 21, determined not to wait any longer, Nat, Henry, and Hark were joined for a supper of pig and brandy in the dark woods near the Travis farm by four other slaves, Sam Francis, Nelson Williams, and Will Francis, Hark Travis's brother-in-law. Will was known to be an expert with an ax, and his owner, Nathaniel Francis, was fond of Nat and had known him since he was a child. The fourth was another new recruit, Jack Reese, the slave of William Reese, who was somewhat hesitant about involving himself in a violent conspiracy.

Like a military officer, Turner saluted his gathered troops as they ate barbecue and made their plans. He asked the slave Will why he had decided to join the group. Will responded that "his life was worth no more than others, and his liberty as dear to him." Will then told Nat that he was willing to give up his life for freedom. That was good enough for Nat, and he welcomed Will into his trusted little band of slave conspirators.

Assuming the title of "General Nat," Turner and his tiny band plotted long into the darkness until they finally agreed to attack the Travis household on that very night. The slaves were to arm and equip themselves, and as Turner recalled, "neither age nor sex was to be spared."

The idea seemed to be that they would go from farm to farm until they "gathered sufficient force." Nat Turner would be the commander-in-chief of a large slave army that he anticipated would join them from neighboring farms and plantations as word of the rebellion spread. He would become his people's Spartacus (a Greek gladiator who led a slave rebellion against Rome between 73 and 71 B.C.) as he led them to the promised land of freedom. Nat Turner's long years of waiting were now over. After August 21, 1831, his name would strike terror and fear into the hearts of whites throughout the slave South for generations to come.[16]

5

Nat Turner's Rebellion: The Fire This Time

If we...do not falter in our duty now, we may be able, handful that we are, to end the racial nightmare, and achieve our country and change the history of the world. If we do not now dare everything, the fulfillment of that prophecy, recreated from the Bible in song by a slave, is upon us: God gave Noah the rainbow sign, No more water, the fire next time!
—James Baldwin,
The Fire Next Time, 1964

Most slaves in Southampton County had no idea that six of their fellow slaves were secretly meeting in the woods near Cabin Pond on August 21, 1831, to plan open rebellion. However, a network existed in which some slaves were well aware of what Nat and his followers were planning. Nelson Williams, one of Nat's lieutenants, had warned his friends on the previous Thursday to "look out and take care of themselves—that something would happen before long."

A slave called Henry testified that on the Saturday preceding "the insurrection," he was told by another slave named Isham "that Genl. Nat was going to rise and murder all the whites." Isham also said he had been threatened with death if he did not join the slave rebels.[1]

Clearly, the network of slave communication reached from farm to farm in the county. Even if most slaves didn't intend to join up with Turner and his band, there is no question that rumors of the plot had gotten around. They may even have extended into adjoining counties on both sides of the Virginia–North Carolina border.

Turner clearly hoped that, as news of his rebellion was passed by word of mouth, other slaves would throw down their hoes and rakes, steal a sword or a rifle, and join his little army. Where he hoped to lead his forces, once they gathered, has been all but lost in the aftermath of what took place over the forty-eight-hour period that began on that dusky morning of Monday, August 22.

This much is known. Nat and his six followers sat around their campfire plotting in the dark woods on Cabin Pond. They ate barbecue and drank apple brandy into the late hours of the warm summer night.

Night gave way to the early morning. One of the band wondered how their revolt would succeed. After all, Jack Reese complained, how could seven poorly armed slaves carry out a large-scale rebellion with any measure of success?

Nat reassured his lieutenants. They had been spreading unrest for months, he told them. He was confident that many blacks would gather to join the slave army as it passed through their vicinity to liberate them.

What was Nat Turner's plan—beyond wholesale violence—once he had gathered a formidable slave army? There is some question here and much disagreement. One theory is that Nat and his army would fight their way into Jerusalem (Courtland, Virginia, today). Jerusalem was the seat or "county town" of Southampton County.

However, Thomas Wentworth Higginson, a leading abolitionist who wrote about the Turner rebellion in 1861, theorized that after Nat raised his troops, he intended to strike terror in the hearts of the whites by retreating into the Dismal Swamp, a large, snake-infested, wooded bog located some 20 miles (32 km) east of the Travis farm. Fugitive slaves had been known to hide there in the past. Perhaps Nat hoped that he and his guerrilla army could raid the Virginia and nearby North Carolina countryside and then retreat to safety, living like the legendary Robin Hood and his Merry Men in the wooded security of their swampy Sherwood Forest.

One argument contends that Nat and his slave army intended to march as far as the port city of Norfolk, where they would seize ships and set sail for their African homeland.[2] This theory, while probably unrealistic, is part of the myth and legend that sprang up around Nat and his band. It probably owes much to the story of the Greek slave Spartacus, who, around 71 B.C., commanded an army of slaves who tried to fight their way down the map of Italy to the port city of Brundusium (now Brindisi). There they planned to pay pirates to ferry them on their fast ships away from Italy and Roman bondage.

Spartacus and seventy slaves training at a gladiator school in Capua escaped to the mountains of Vesuvius in south-central Italy and raided the adjoining towns for food and arms. They issued a call for the slaves of Italy to join them and soon had an army of seventy thousand men. Eventually, dissension hit the slave ranks, and Spartacus had to face the fact that some in his slave army were interested only in looting and pillaging the towns and villages. With his forces split, Spartacus faced two Roman legions. The slaves were defeated, Spartacus himself was killed, and thousands of slaves were captured. Then six thousand slaves were crucified along the Appian Way from Capua to Rome, and their bodies were left to rot for months as an example to any slave contemplating rebellion.

Nat himself offers history nothing of his plan, if he had one. He merely said, "We remained at the feast, until about two hours in the night when we went to the house." The house Nat mentions was the house of his new master, Joseph Travis.

Nat picks up the story in chilling detail. The slaves arrived at the Travis property and were greeted by a slave named Austin. The group, except for Nat, stopped to drink some cider. Afraid to arouse anyone in the neighborhood by the loud noise caused by breaking down the door with an ax, Nat recalled, "we determined to enter the house secretly, and murder them whilst sleeping." The Travis family attended church services that evening and had arrived home around midnight. They were all sleeping soundly when Nat and his band arrived in the darkness a few hours later. It was around 2 A.M.[3]

The slave Hark got a ladder, and set it up against the chimney. Nat himself climbed through a second-floor window, then went downstairs to open the door for his troops. After taking Travis's guns, Nat went upstairs to the room of his sleeping master, where he hit Travis in the head with a hatchet. But Nat's blow was hardly enough to kill or even silence Joseph Travis. The dazed man sprang from his bed shouting out to his sleeping wife. They were to be Joseph Travis's last words and the opening scene of Nat Turner's rebellion. The slave Will Francis, of whom little is known except that he obviously had a pen-

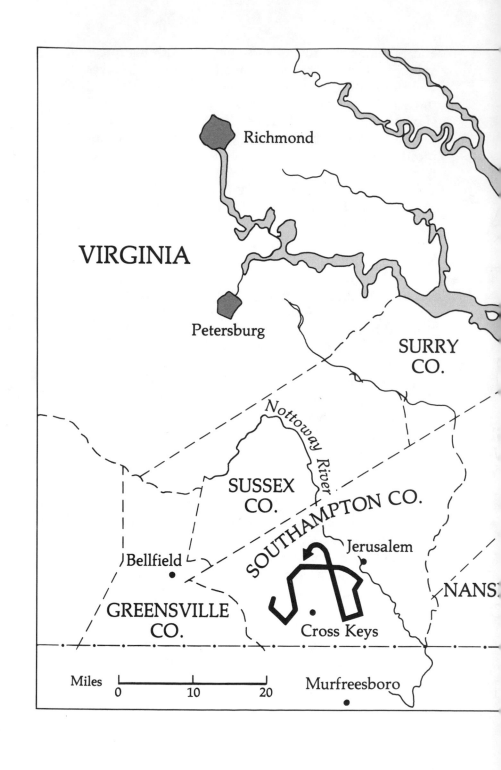

Richmond

VIRGINIA

Petersburg

SURRY
CO.

Nottoway River

SUSSEX
CO.

SOUTHAMPTON CO.

Jerusalem

Bellfield

NANS

GREENSVILLE
CO.

Cross Keys

Miles

0   10   20

Murfreesboro

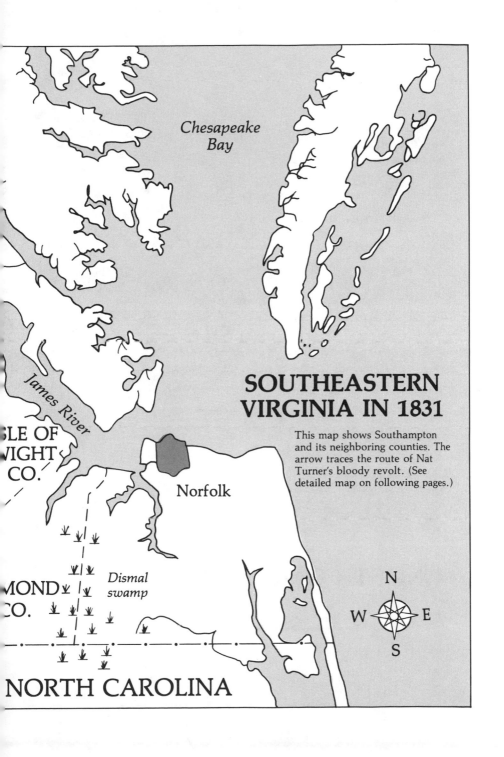

Chesapeake
Bay

James River

ISLE OF
WIGHT
CO.

Norfolk

SOUTHEASTERN
VIRGINIA IN 1831

This map shows Southampton and its neighboring counties. The arrow traces the route of Nat Turner's bloody revolt. (See detailed map on following pages.)

MOND
CO.

Dismal
swamp

N

W ✦ E

S

NORTH CAROLINA

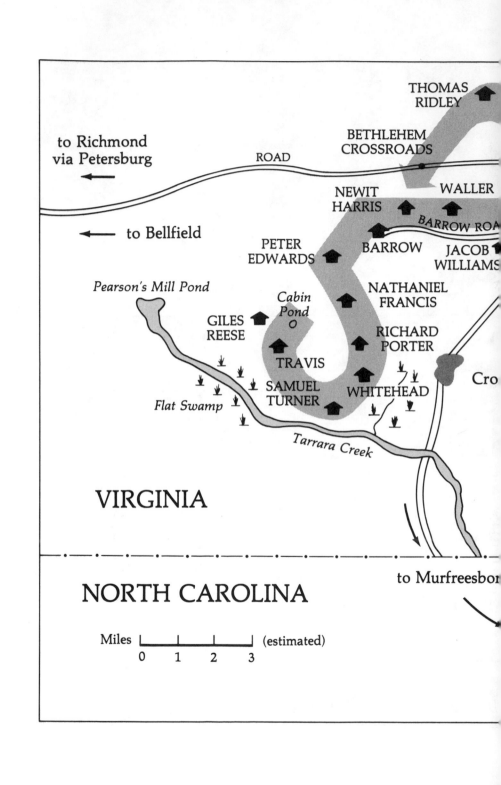

THOMAS
RIDLEY

to Richmond
via Petersburg

ROAD

BETHLEHEM
CROSSROADS

WALLER

NEWIT
HARRIS

to Bellfield

BARROW ROA

PETER
EDWARDS

BARROW

JACOB
WILLIAMS

Pearson's Mill Pond

Cabin
Pond

NATHANIEL
FRANCIS

GILES
REESE

RICHARD
PORTER

TRAVIS

Cro

Flat Swamp

SAMUEL
TURNER

WHITEHEAD

Tarrara Creek

VIRGINIA

NORTH CAROLINA

to Murfreesbor

Miles

0   1   2   3

(estimated)

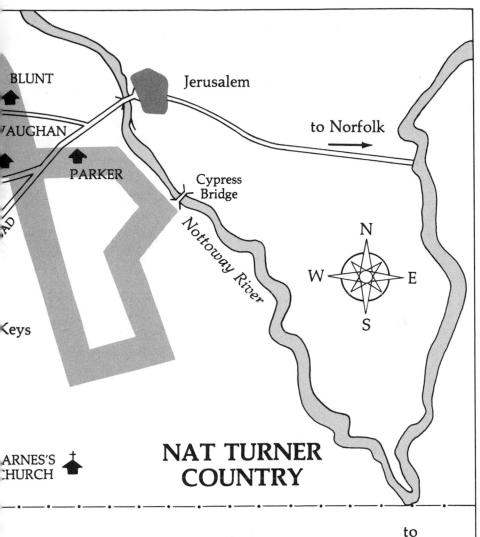

BLUNT

VAUGHAN

PARKER

Jerusalem

to Norfolk

Cypress
Bridge

Nottoway River

Keys

N
W E
S

ARNES'S
CHURCH

NAT TURNER
COUNTRY

This map of the southwestern part of Southampton County shows
many of the houses and farms mentioned in this chapter that fell in
the path (shaded arrow) of Nat Turner's rebellious campaign.

to

Dismal
Swamp

chant for violence, finished Travis off, hacking him to pieces. Then he turned his ax on Joseph's wife, Sally Travis. She was hacked to death as she lay in bed. Within a few moments two of the children, including young Putnam Moore, were murdered as they slept. As Nat remembered the bloody events of that early Monday morning, "The murder of this family, five in number, was the work of a moment, not one of them awoke; there was a little infant sleeping in a cradle, that was forgotten until we had left the house and gone some distance, when Henry and Will returned and killed it."[4]

With the deaths of the Travises and Putnam Moore, Nat Turner no longer had a master. Technically, for the first time in his life, he was a free man.

The slaves took four guns and a few old rifles from the Travis house, along with a few pounds of gunpowder. For a while they lingered around the Travis barn, where Nat, like any general, drilled his victorious troops until he was confident that they were prepared to march into the next battle.

The group's leaders also took steps to avoid defections. After the Travis murders one slave, Jack Reese, complained that he was too ill to continue. However, Hark forced the frightened slave to remain with the group as they went to their next target. The farm of Salathul Francis, the Travises' neighbor, was located 600 yards (540 m) from the Travis place. The slaves made their way in silence in the stillness of the night. As one writer described their movements, "Swift and stealthy as Indians, the black men passed from house to house—not pausing, not hesitating, as their terrible work went on."[5]

Sam and Will knocked on the door of the house, and when Salathul Francis came to the door, Sam told him that he had come to deliver a letter. As he opened the door, the unsuspecting Francis was dragged out of the house and, Nat said, "dispatched by repeated blows to the head."

As there were no other whites on the Francis property, the slaves then moved quietly on to the next farm, owned by Mrs. Piety Reese. Finding the door unlocked, they entered the house and murdered Mrs. Reese in her bed as she slept. Her son William, awakened by the noisy commotion, had time only to sleepily ask who was there before he too was killed. At the Reese house their former slave, Jack Reese, who had panicked back at the Travis farm, regained his composure and, apparently his boldness. After putting on his dead master's shoes and socks, Jack stepped over William Reese's bleeding body to join his comrades as they slashed the Reese family's overseer. The overseer became one of the few survivors who lived to talk about that violent Virginia morning.

The events of the rebellion had gotten off to a bloody start. But violence for violence's sake was not, Nat later said, the ultimate objective of his rebellion. Turner wanted to strike fear into the hearts of the whites and thought he could use terror to spread the alarm that a massive slave rebellion was fully underway. He reportedly said that "women and children would afterwards have been spared, and men too who ceased to resist."[6]

It was sunrise when the rebels arrived at the farm of Nat's former mistress, Elizabeth Turner. Until they reached the Turner farm, the slaves had continued to operate quietly in the still darkness of the early morning Virginia countryside. Their victims had either been stabbed or axed to death. No shots had been fired to shatter the quiet or to arouse anyone who might have been able to escape for help.

Nat and his little army had bypassed the modest farm of Giles Reese (no relation to Mrs. Piety Reese). Most probably, Nat was thinking about his own family. He wanted to spare his wife and young children, who still lived on the Reese place, the agony of watching their master and his family murdered in cold blood. There is also evidence that Nat's wife had some inkling that her husband was planning something. During the previous week Nat had given her some papers that contained a list of his followers and a few of his mystical drawings.

For years Nat had harbored great resentment toward his former mistress. He recalled that it was Elizabeth Turner who had sold the Turner family to two masters, thus forever separating them and shattering any semblance of a normal family life. Samuel Turner's widow had prospered in the years since she sold Nat and her other slaves to Giles Reese and Thomas Moore. Still living alone as a widow, Mrs. Turner now had eighteen slaves and an overseer. The sun of the new morning had just risen as Nat signaled his men to attack the Turner house.

The first man killed was Hartwell Peebles, the Turners' overseer, who must have been surprised to find the slaves gathering at the farm's distillery so early in the morning. A slave by the name of Austin shot the startled overseer by the still.

Once again, Turner called upon the strength of Will, who used his ax to break down the door of the house. The slaves entered the house and found Elizabeth Turner and her neighbor, Mrs. Sarah Newsome, cowering in the middle of the room—Nat recalled—"almost frightened to death." Will turned his ax on Mrs. Turner, killing her almost instantly. Nat, now armed with a long sword, grabbed Mrs. Newsome by the hand and tried to kill her by hitting her over the head with his sword. But Nat's sword was dull, and it was up to Will to finish her off.

After looting the Turner household, Nat took stock of his growing army which had increased to fifteen, with nine of the slaves mounted on horseback.

Armed with an odd assortment of guns, clubs, swords, axes, and farm tools, Nat decided to exercise his military authority by splitting their forces. Hark took six men and went to the Bryant farm while Nat and Will led the men with horses to the Whitehead plantation.

Catherine Whitehead was a socially prominent widow with a son Richard—a young Methodist minister who had only the day before preached at the local church—and two daughters, Margaret and Harriet. As Turner and his men rode up to the Whitehead plantation, they came upon young Richard Whitehead as he stood working with some slaves in a cotton field. Some of the slaves, sensing that trouble had ridden up to the Whitehead farm, ran off. When they returned, everyone in the Whitehead household was dead. Two of Whitehead's slaves, Jack and Andrew, then rode to the nearby house of a free black named Thomas Hathcock. They told Hathcock about the massacre and, according to Hathcock's testimony later in court, were "much grieved." What Andrew and Jack had seen must have been terrifying.

Richard Whitehead begged Nat for his life. But Nat had no compassion for the young preacher. With the other rebels chanting for blood, Will took his ax to Richard Whitehead and savagely killed him. The group then surrounded the Whitehead house. As the Whitehead family's slaves watched in horror, Turner and his men systematically slaughtered the family. Three women of the household and a grandchild were killed. The rebels ran around inside the house looking for the other women. An old slave, Hubbard, refused to open the door to a bedroom and tried to convince Turner's men that he was alone and too frightened to let them in. Actually, in the chaos, Hubbard had hidden Harriet Whitehead under the bed.

Meanwhile, Nat had chased a woman into the nearby garden. When he found that she was just a frightened slave, he let her go and returned to the house. Nat says, "As I came round to the door I saw Will pulling Mrs. Whitehead out of the house, and at the step he nearly severed her head from her body, with his broad ax."[7]

Margaret Whitehead was hiding by the cellar when Nat found her. She fled in terror as he approached. But Nat caught up with her in a nearby field and slashed her over and over again with his sword. Finally, Nat picked up a fence rail and beat her to death. Margaret Whitehead was the first person Nat had killed that hot August morning.

After the Whitehead massacre, the slaves held a meeting in the yard. The six men led by Hark rejoined the group and reported that they had killed everyone in Henry Bryant's family. Nat drew a battle plan in the dirt. Once again the slave forces would split up. Hark's group was assigned to go on foot to the farms of Howell Harris and Trajan Doyle. The second group, a mounted cavalry led by Nat, would go to the homes of Will's master, Nathaniel Francis, and Richard Porter. After killing the whites on these farms and recruiting more black soldiers, Nat planned to reunite his forces and drive to the county seat in Jerusalem.

When Turner and his men left the Whitehead farm, Hubbard took his terrified mistress and hid her in the woods. But poor Harriet Whitehead, who had just witnessed the slaughter of her entire family, was not thinking clearly. Fearing that Hubbard would betray her to the rebels, she ran deeper into the woods and would not come out when the old slave returned with food. She was found later by a search party of whites as she wandered dazed and muddy through the mosquito-infested woods. She alone survived the Whitehead family massacre.

Meanwhile, the killings continued. The slaves met Trajan Doyle on the road to his farm and killed him. Turner led his men on horseback down a dirt road toward the small farm of Richard Porter. But by now slaves who remained loyal to their masters had ridden from farm to farm to warn some of the neighboring families that a revolt was taking place in the area. The Porter family had escaped into the woods, and Nat realized "that the alarm had already spread."[8]

Nat instructed Will to take the other men on horseback to the area of the Nathaniel Francis farm while he rode off to gather up the slaves he had sent on foot down the road to the Doyle farm. He knew that his work had been betrayed by other slaves but there was little he could do about that serious problem. The major immediate task before him was to unite his forces and regroup before the local militia was called out for battle.

The group of slaves led by Will and Sam Francis arrived next at the farm of their master, Nathaniel Francis. A short time before they rode up, at around eight o'clock, Francis had just finished his breakfast when a young slave came running toward him down the road near his house. Francis knew that the slave belonged to his sister on the Travis farm which was only 2 or 3 miles (4–5 km) away. The young boy was visibly upset as he told Francis, "Some folks, some folks have killed all the white folks."[9]

Nathaniel Francis could hardly believe what he heard. "You don't know what you're talking about," he replied. But then he saw that the boy was terrified and quite upset. So he immediately returned to his own house to tell the women. Then he left for the Travis farm to investigate. His mother, worried that something terrible had happened to her daughter, Sally Travis, decided to take a shortcut to the Travis place and left on foot. Remaining behind were Francis's pregnant wife, Lavinia, two young nephews, the overseer Henry Doyle, and the household's slaves—except for Will and Sam.

As the familiar figures of Will and Sam

approached the Francis farm, Nathaniel Francis's little nephew, only three years old, ran down the road to offer the slaves a cheerful greeting as they rode up. Will decapitated the child with his ax while the other rebels killed his screaming brother, who had been hiding in the barnyard nearby.

The family slaves scattered in every direction, shouting and shrieking. Their overseer, Henry Doyle, ran for the house to warn the women. When he came out, he was immediately shot dead. Will and Sam then ran for the house, where they hoped to find Nathaniel Francis. The slaves inside told them that Francis had gone off with his wife. But Lavinia Francis was being hidden upstairs in a closet by a slave named Nelson. Fortunately, she fainted and missed the bloodcurdling scene that was taking place around her house.

Will and Sam searched the house and, finding nothing, ran outside, where they spotted a white woman with a child down the road. Mrs. John K. Williams, the wife of the local schoolteacher, had come to spend the day with the ladies on the Francis farm after her husband had left for school. The sight that greeted Mrs. Williams that morning froze her in her tracks. Two slaves were running toward her with axes. After killing Mrs. Williams and her child, the slaves celebrated by drinking brandy from the family still while they did their best to enlist more slaves into their growing army. A slave by the name of Dred joined the rebels, but others had to be forced into the band as hostages. One slave who refused to go with them was disabled by having his heelstrings cut so that he couldn't alert anyone.[10]

Meanwhile, John "Choctaw" Williams, who lived near the Whitehead farm, had heard screams that morning. The young teacher decided to investigate. Upon entering the Whitehead house, Williams found the grisly remains of the Turner band's work. He found Mrs. Whitehead, her headless son, and her daughter murdered in her bedroom. Almost overcome by the bloody scene, Williams ran out to the road. He was on his way to warn his family when he ran into one of his own young slaves. The boy told him that his wife and child had been murdered. Finding his murdered family, the grief-stricken Williams ran into the woods, hid for a while, and then started off for Murfreesboro, North Carolina, to alert the governor's troops.[11]

By this time word of the slave rampage had begun to spread through the county. It must be remembered that the Turner rebellion took place before the invention of the telegraph. Thus, the early news was carried from Southampton County during the earliest hours of the violence by human messengers and by whatever network existed on the slave grapevine from small farms to the larger plantations. It is therefore not at all surprising that many unsubstantiated rumors began to circulate in and around Southampton County by midmorning on August 22. One rumor had it that the British had invaded and were killing the whites.

In the county seat of Jerusalem the citizens barricaded the bridge across the Nottoway River in a panic when they heard that an army of five hundred slaves was on its way to slaughter them. Church bells tolled throughout the countryside as frenzied riders were sent out to give the alarm or to fetch the local militia. In Jerusalem women locked their doors, hid their children, and shivered in fear as the town's church bells rang throughout the steamy day.

It took nearly an entire day for Governor John Floyd to receive word of the insurrection in Richmond. Justice James Trezevant of the Southampton County Court had managed to get a message off to the authorities by express rider. Trezevant asked that a large military force be sent with enough arms and men to crush the revolt.

The next day, August 23, Governor Floyd noted in his diary that he received Trezevant's message. He wrote: "Upon receipt of this information, I began to consider how to prepare for the crisis. To call out the militia and equip a military force for that service." Ironically, Floyd, a former congressman, opposed slavery because he believed it to be a barrier to the economic growth and development he sought for Virginia.[12]

Meanwhile, Nat Turner was desperately trying to catch up with his divided forces. The cavalry, led by Will, continued their bloody work as they rode from farm to farm. From the Francis farm they went to the farm of Peter Edwards, but news of their actions had preceded them, and Edwards had escaped with his entire family. They then galloped down the Barrow Road toward the farm of John T. Barrow. The Barrow Road ran due east for 5 miles (8 km), then intersected the main road that went south to Murfreesboro, North Carolina, or northeast to the county seat in Jerusalem.

John T. Barrow, a grizzled veteran of the War of 1812, had heard the rumors of a slave uprising that morning. But he didn't believe them. When Will's horsemen came galloping up to his farm that morning, Barrow was working in a cotton field. The old man bravely tried to fight the slaves off and engaged them in hand-to-hand combat. His valiant struggle was enough to give his wife time to escape. Riding hard to catch up to his tiny army, Nat arrived at the Barrow place to find the old man in the field with his throat cut. The slaves, impressed by Barrow's courage, had wrapped his body in a quilt and placed a plug of tobacco on his chest.[13]

When Nat finally caught up with his men at the home of Captain Newit Harris, they cheered as he rode up. Some of them were in the yard loading their guns. Others, angry that the Harris family had escaped, looted the house and raided the brandy cellar. Nat found them drinking in the yard. His band had now increased to about forty. It was between nine and ten o'clock in the morning when Nat ordered his troops to mount up and march. It appeared that General Nat was intent on moving his army toward Jerusalem.

Two miles (3 km) down the road the slaves, pushing their horses, rode up to the farm of Levi Waller. Nat, lost in his thoughts, had taken a position to the rear of his troops, deciding to "place fifteen or twenty of the best armed and most to be relied on, in front." Nat said that because of this tactic he never got to the next house until after the murders there were committed. By the time Nat rode up to the Waller farm, the rebels had slaughtered ten children and Mrs. Waller. As he recalled,

I sometimes got in sight in time to see the work of death completed, viewed the mangled bodies as they lay, in silent satisfaction, and immediately started in quest of other victims.[14]

Levi Waller, unable to arm himself before the slaves were upon them, hid himself in the weeds behind his garden on the opposite side of the house. Poor Waller could hear the screams of the children and the shouts of the rebels. He crept closer to the house and witnessed the murder of his wife and children. Overcome with rage and grief, Waller then ran into a nearby swamp. After a while he returned to the house, and from his hiding place in the family plum orchard behind the garden, he could see Nat Turner wearing an old hat and a long silver sword sitting astride his stolen horse. Nat appeared to be in full command of the slaves who, Waller later testified, "were drinking."[15]

In addition to Waller, William Crocker, the local schoolmaster, two of Waller's sons, and a small girl who had luckily hidden in the chimney also escaped the fury of Turner's angry men.

Finally, two groups of whites were organized to move out to the Barrow Road to stop Turner and his men. One force, numbering about forty men, was led by a Jerusalem lawyer, William C. Parker. Ironically, Parker was later assigned by the court to act as Nat Turner's defense counsel. Parker and his men picked up Turner's trail at the Newit Harris plantation and followed it along the Barrow Road. They found one family after another that had been massacred by the marauding slave rebels.

A second force of about twenty men was led by Captain Arthur Middleton of the Southampton County militia. Middleton's force reached the Waller farm about fifteen minutes after the raiders. What they found made them sick to their stomachs. Ten decapitated children were piled in "one bleeding heap," and another child, badly slashed, was still alive. The militia men placed her under a tree, where she soon died. Middleton was so upset that he could not go on. He returned home to protect his own family.

With two separate forces hot on their trail and word of their violent work rapidly spreading, Turner and his men started to find one abandoned farm after another as they made their way down the Barrow Road. But not all of the whites along the Barrow Road were fortunate enough to receive news of the insurrection or a warning that an army of slaves was rampaging in their direction.

The wife and three children of Jacob Williams; the family of Caswell Worrell, the Williamses' overseer; a young man named Edwin Drury, and the unsuspecting widow Rebecca Vaughan and her pretty eighteen-year-old niece, Anne Elizabeth, all fell to the guns and axes of the onrushing Turner marauders. Mrs. Vaughan had retreated to her house and bolted the door when the slaves surrounded the house. She begged them to take whatever they wanted and to spare her and her niece's lives. But a slave shot her in the face through the closed window. They broke into the house as Anne Elizabeth rushed downstairs, and they shot her too. Then they killed the overseer and one of Mrs. Vaughan's sons.

At this point Nat's army had increased to fifty or sixty men, all mounted and armed with guns, axes, swords and clubs. Nat decided to head for Jerusalem. "My object," he said, "was to reach there as soon as possible."[16]

When they reached the farm of James W. Parker, only about 3 miles (5 km) from Jerusalem, Nat wanted to push on because he knew that Parker was away in Jerusalem. But some of the slaves apparently had a score to settle, and they prevailed on Turner to allow them to attack the Parker house. Nat stayed by the gate with seven or eight of his men while the rest crossed the field to the Parker house half a mile (804 m) away.

Turner grew impatient and went to hurry his men. On their return to the road they were attacked by a group of eighteen whites who had been hastily organized. Turner quickly rallied his troops, ordering them to return the fire of the whites and then to charge them. The blacks were firing as the whites retreated into a field with Turner and his men in hot pursuit. Turner thought he had the small band of militia on the run as he and his men chased them about 200 yards (180 m) over a small hill. But the retreating whites were saved from disaster when, at the last minute, a troop of volunteers from Jerusalem rode up.

Upon hearing the gunfire from the field, the reinforcements were able to prevent Turner and his men from slaughtering their opponents. Several of

Turner's men had been wounded. Others began to panic and run away. Hark, one of Nat's key lieutenants, had his horse shot out from under him.

Nat realized that he was defeated at Parker's field and that any attempt to march farther along the Barrow Road toward Jerusalem would end in disaster. With the remaining members of his now-scattered forces, he crossed the Cypress Bridge on the Nottoway River, hoping that somehow they could reach Jerusalem another way and attack the town from the rear. Nat figured that the whites would be looking for him to try to regroup along the Barrow Road. He also knew that if he was going to continue his rebellion with any measure of success, he had to somehow reach Jerusalem to get arms and ammunition.

However, after traveling a short distance with only about twenty men, he found a few more of his followers. They told him that his slave army had "dispersed in every direction." Nat said, "After trying in vain to collect a sufficient force to proceed to Jerusalem, I determined to return, as I was sure they would make back to their old neighborhood, where they would rejoin me, make new recruits and come down again."[17]

But Nat was wrong. Though he did not know it, for all intents and purposes his bloody rebellion was over. The most commonly cited number of whites killed in the span of those forty-eight hours is fifty-seven. However, Nat's *Confessions*, published in 1831, includes a list that totals fifty-five. Half of those killed were children. On one farm alone, there was a school where the slaves murdered ten children. None of the children has ever been listed by name. There is also some additional evidence that a man, twenty-four-year-old Shepherd Lee, was killed. Lee's name does not appear on any published list.

In addition, the homes of the murdered farmers were ransacked. A few historians wrongly claim that no looting took place. Some money and valuables *were* taken from the farms and plantations. However, it is true that most of the goods taken by the slaves were things they needed to support their revolt: horses, guns, and ammunition. No farms were burned, and according to published reports, not a single female victim was molested.

For Nat Turner and his slave rebels, the defeat in Parker's field was the beginning of the end.[18]

6

The Fire Burns Out: Escape, Capture, Trial, and Execution

The right of man to the enjoyment of freedom is a settled point; and where he is deprived of this, without any criminal act of his own, it is his duty to regain his liberty at every cost.... Every eye is now turned towards the south, looking for another Nat Turner.

—William Wells Brown, 1863

On Thursday, August 25, 1831, John Hampden Pleasants, the senior editor of *The Constitutional Whig*, a newspaper published in Richmond, described what he had seen in and around Southampton County. Pleasants had gone from Richmond to Southampton County, both as a member of the militia and as a journalist. He was the only newspaperman who actually visited the chaotic scene.

Arriving in Jerusalem from Petersburg, the young editor found much of the countryside virtually deserted by the white farmers. Pleasants wrote: "We found the whole country thoroughly alarmed; every

man armed, the dwellings all deserted
inhabitants; and the farms most gener
possession of the blacks."

Pleasants goes on to describe som
ders and lists sixty-two as the number of w
killed. Noting correctly that the killings began at the
home of Mr. Travis, he went on to write: "A negro,
called captain [sic] Moore, and who it is added is a
preacher, is the reputed leader."[1]

Clearly, after a week had gone by, the facts of Nat
Turner's violent activities were still trickling in to the
authorities and the frightened populace in an irregu-
lar and distorted fashion. News traveled slowly if not
unevenly during Turner's time, and the public rarely
got an accurate picture of what was going on. This
heightened anxieties, increased fear and panic, and
promoted widespread unrest. One militia volunteer
from Norfolk wrote a letter to the *American Beacon*
stating that his troop had taken twelve men and one
woman as prisoners, "together with the head of the
celebrated Nelson [Nat's lieutenant], called by the
blacks, 'Gen. Nelson.'" The excited militiaman went
on to write that, "Hark (the black's abbreviation of
Herculeus) and Gen. Nat…have also been shot and
taken prisoners: in fact almost all the ring leaders,
with the exception of the Prophet, have been either
taken or killed." Of course, the writer of the letter was
somewhat confused since "General Nat" and "the
Prophet" were one and the same person. And not
only was General Nat not shot, he wasn't taken pris-
oner. At least not yet.[2]

The failure of Nat's revolt can be traced to three
factors. First, the blacks were poorly armed and had
almost totally run out of ammunition. Second, as the
slaves rode from farm to farm, too many of them
stopped to help themselves to the abundant cider
stills and brandy cellars of the white farmers. As a

result, to put it bluntly, they were either too drunk or too tired to fight. Third, and perhaps most important, blacks did not flock to join the slave army as Nat had hoped they would. It wasn't that the slaves were unsympathetic with what Nat was trying to do. They just didn't believe that he could succeed. Thus, aside from the slaves who remained steadfastly loyal to their masters by hiding them or even physically defending them, most slaves just stood on the sidelines and watched silently, hoping, perhaps, that Nat and his tiny slave army might somehow succeed against the overwhelming odds that faced them.

At the most, Nat Turner's slave army may have numbered sixty men. Without soldiers it is, ultimately, impossible to fight a war of any duration. Without enough guns, ammunition, or troops, Nat's war against the white slaveowners of Southampton County was doomed. As one historian wrote, "had Nat Turner been successful in capturing Jerusalem, with its arms and ammunition, he might have pro- longed the conflict for many days; perhaps, with guerrilla warfare, for weeks."[3] But this was not to be. The rumor circulating in Southampton County that Nat had raised an army of between a thousand and twelve hundred men was just that: a rumor.

Though Nat and the remnant of his scattered forces raided more farms during the course of the late afternoon of August 22, they found that the whites had fled and that the farms were deserted. Finally, as night fell, the tired rebels reached the plantation of Major Thomas Ridley, where they hoped to recruit reinforcements from among Ridley's 145 slaves.

Once again Nat was to be disappointed. The Ridley farm was already guarded by the militia, and Nat was forced to withdraw his men into the nearby woods for the night after only four of Ridley's slaves had joined his forces. Nat gave the order to place sentinels and then the exhausted leader tried to get some sleep, hoping that the dawn of a new day would change his little army's fortunes. However, during the night Nat was awakened by a commotion and, to his dismay, found that one of the sentinels had sounded an alarm that the slaves were about to be attacked. As a result, almost half of his men ran off in different directions. Nat was to face August 23 with his forces cut down to twenty men.

At daybreak Nat and his men approached the farm of Dr. Simon Blunt, again hoping to get some of the slaves to join them.

But Blunt had been warned and was ready for a fight. As they rode up to the house, Hark shouted and fired his gun to see if anybody was home. They were surprised when their fire was immediately returned. This was to be the scene of Nat's final battle. Blunt, his son, and a few white men were armed and waiting for Turner and his men. Their guns were loaded. Blunt even armed his slaves with farm implements, stationing them near the kitchen door of the main house so that they could see the lane that connected to the main road. As Nat, Hark, and the others approached, they were met by a heavy burst of gunfire and forced to retreat. Turner lost several more of his men, including Hark, who was wounded and captured. Nat said later, "I do not know what became of them, as I never saw them afterwards."[4]

With his forces in almost total disarray, Nat decided to return to the area where he had begun his rebellion near the home of Captain Newit Harris. Moving through the woods Nat, Will, and his remaining men could hear the shouts of men and the barking of dogs from the Barrow Road. Armed bands of whites were roving throughout the area in search of the rebel slaves. From the woods Nat could see that the militia had already arrived at the Harris farm.

Finally, the whites saw the slaves on the edge of the forest and opened fire on Nat and his men with their rifles. When the smoke cleared, Will and two of Nat's men lay dead. Nat was left with two men, Jacob and another slave named Nat. The three slaves ran off into the woods and hid until nightfall. Nat then sent his last two men off in search of Henry, Sam, Nelson and Hark, hoping that somehow he could rally his troops once again. He set their original spot in Cabin Woods as the place where they would all meet. But by the next day, with white patrols everywhere, Nat gave up hope that his last two soldiers would ever return. Fearing that he would be betrayed, Nat said, "I gave up all hope for the present; and on Thursday night after having supplied myself with provisions from Mr. Travis's, I scratched a hole under a pile of fence rails in a field, where I concealed myself for six weeks, never leaving my hiding place but for a few minutes in the dead of night to get water which was very near."[5]

As news of the Turner insurrection began spreading all over Virginia between Monday night and Tuesday morning of August 22–23, the first official response was somewhat muddled. Poor Governor Floyd was bound by a rule of the state constitution that required him to seek the advice and approval of the Governor's Council before he could call up the state militia. Floyd found the members of the council off on vacation. In fact, not one council member was in Richmond. Floyd complained in his diary about his situation, writing, "I must first require advice of Council, and then disregard it, if I please." Finally, with the approval of the lieutenant governor, himself a member of the council, Governor Floyd sent out riders in all directions to call up his state militia for duty in Southampton County.

Floyd did not have to worry just about the Turner revolt. Rumors arose all over the city about hundreds of blacks rising up and murdering their masters.

People gathered on the streets and in the parks of the city. The rumors grew worse as word hit Richmond that a huge army of blacks had been seen moving out of the Dismal Swamp and heading in the direction of the city. Barricades appeared along the main roads to Petersburg, Norfolk, and Richmond. Armed patrols of anxiety-ridden white men galloped through the streets of the cities seeking revenge on any black person unlucky enough to stumble in their path. Innocent blacks were arrested, and many were even killed on the spot. Big cities and small towns throughout Virginia were in a state of frenzied uproar. Southern whites had claimed for years that their slaves were "happy." They not only failed to convince others, they hadn't convinced themselves, as proved by their hysterical reaction that a general uprising among the slaves was about to sweep through the state.

On August 29, *The American Beacon*, published in Norfolk, assured its worried readers that "from all we can learn there appears to have been no contact with blacks in any other part of the state." However, it did not matter. As word spread about the brutal murders of the whites in Southampton County by their slaves, many whites decided to take the law into their own hands.

Finally, three companies of federal troops from Fort Monroe were sent to protect the worried citizens of Norfolk. On August 24, the commander of the militia sent to Jerusalem, General Richard Eppes, wrote to the governor assuring him that everything was under control and requesting that the troops be directed to return. As Eppes noted, "The insurgents are nearly dispersed. Fifteen have been killed and twelve are in jail." Eppes told the governor that he had taken forty-eight prisoners.[6]

But everything was hardly under control. By August 28, General Eppes felt that it was necessary to issue a military order to warn the white citizens of the region that continued acts of unjustified violence against blacks "shall be punished, if necessary, by the articles of war." White vigilantes on horseback rode through the backwoods, into the swamps and down the country lanes of southeastern Virginia, looking for fugitive rebels or any black remotely associated with the Turner uprising. Innocent blacks, slave and free, lost their lives in the following days.

John Hampden Pleasants reported "the slaughter of many blacks without trial, and under circumstances of great barbarity." By September 3, Pleasants estimated that perhaps more than 40 innocent blacks had lost their lives to the violent mobs that were seeking revenge as they rode through the county. Pleasants met one white man who boasted that he had killed between ten and fifteen blacks.

John W. Cromwell, a black writer who taught school in Southampton County after the Civil War, interviewed a number of blacks who recalled the Turner rebellion and who were still alive during Reconstruction. Cromwell recorded their comments, noting that "a reign of terror followed in Virginia...in a little more than one day 120 Negroes were killed.... Volunteer whites rode in all directions visiting plantations. Negroes were tortured to death, burned, maimed and subjected to nameless atrocities. Slaves who were distrusted were pointed out and if they endeavored to escape, they were ruthlessly shot down."[7]

An unknown black man was caught and beheaded by a gang of whites at the crossroads of the Barrow Road and Jerusalem Highway. The whites put his head on a road post and the marker became known as Blackhead Signpost. In another case, a group of white riders left Richmond for Southampton County with the express purpose of killing every black person they met on the way. As they rode into Southampton County, they came upon a free black working in his field. Someone called out to the man,

"Is this Southampton County?" "Yes sir," the black man replied, "you have just crossed the line by yonder tree." They shot him to death and rode on.[8]

At another level, the relationship between master and slave would be forever changed. Could any master, no matter how decently he treated his slaves, ever go to sleep at night comfortable with the knowledge that his slaves might rise up in the middle of the night and murder him and his family as they slept? After all, the news reports said that Nat Turner had not been badly treated by Joseph Travis. The whites who knew Turner could only say that he was a "shrewd fellow" who "reads, writes and preaches."

Whites were clearly worried about their slaves who, they wanted very much to believe, lived and worked with them in peaceful tranquillity and harmony. On August 29, when a committee composed of Southampton County citizens wrote President Andrew Jackson about the rebellion, they revealed much about the fear that was rapidly spreading through Virginia and the rest of the white South after Nat Turner's rebellion. They wrote, in part:

So inhuman has been the butchery, so indiscriminate the carnage, that the tomahawk and scalping knife have now no horrors.... In the bosom of almost every family the enemy still exists.[9]

Writing on September 26, the Richmond editor John Hampden Pleasants reported that Turner's wife had been located and, after being lashed, had given up some of Nat's papers. The papers were filled with mystical markings and offered little clue to why Nat led such a violent rebellion without any mercy for even women or children. Pleasants reported that Nat's papers conveyed "no definite meaning" and that Nat had once been whipped by his master for saying that blacks ought to be free. Pleasants was also convinced that Nat had left the state. However, many of the whites he interviewed still felt that Nat was somewhere "lurking in his neighbourhood." Indeed, it appeared that Southampton County would never return to normal until the man described by the newspapers as the head of "the banditti" was safely locked away in chains.[10]

Meanwhile, Nat Turner managed successfully to elude capture by the authorities as he hid in the swamps and woods near the Travis farm. Governor Floyd issued a proclamation offering a $500 reward for Turner's capture, accompanied by a complete physical description of Nat that was sent to the governor by William C. Parker of Jerusalem on September 14. It is the most accurate description of Nat Turner on record and was acquired by questioning blacks and whites who knew Nat from the time he was a child:

He is between 30 & 35 years old—5 feet six or 8 inches [165–170 cm] high—weighs between 150 & 160 [67–72 kg] rather bright complexion but not a mulatto—broad-shouldered—large flat nose—large eyes—broad flat feet rather knock kneed—walk brisk and active—hair on the top of the head very thin—no beard except on the upper lip and the tip of the chin. A scar on one of his temples produced by the kick of a mule—also one on the back of his neck by a bite—a large knot on one of the bones of his right arm near the wrist produced by a blow—[11]

While Nat was in hiding, southern justice began to move swiftly for Nat's friends and former soldiers. On August 31, the court convened in Jerusalem to begin the trials of the slaves who had taken part in Nat's rebellion. No jury would hear these cases, which were given over to several judges appointed by

Governor Floyd and his council. They alone would decide the guilt or the innocence of the accused slaves. In light of the hysterical atmosphere that prevailed in Southampton County, the authorities were determined to make it appear that the blacks received a fair trial .

In addition, there were property rights to consider since somebody owned every slave who was brought to trial and the state would ultimately have to pay the owner of every slave who was sentenced to death. With field hands going for anywhere from $400 to $600, the costs were something that had to be considered. Worried that the accused blacks might be lynched by an angry mob, the county authorities asked General Eppes to provide soldiers to guard the jail during the trial.

The court appointed William C. Parker, Thomas R. Gray, and James L. French to defend the accused slaves. The lawyers received $10 per case. That was hardly a generous fee, especially since these men risked their careers if not their personal safety by daring to defend the black rebels who were so despised and vilified throughout the county and the state.

Testimony was offered by blacks as well as whites. The verdict of the court was hardly a model of fairness. For example, the three young slaves of the Francis family were sentenced to death for conspiracy and insurrection even though the testimony indicated that they were forced into joining Turner and his men at gunpoint. Governor Floyd eventually commuted their death sentences, and they were deported from the United States.

Although the major trials took place in the Southampton County Court in Jerusalem, there were other counties in Virginia during this period that held slave trials where blacks were accused of some knowledge of or connection to the Turner revolt. In most cases it was white panic, not black rebellion, that led to the epidemic of trials that took place in Virginia following the Turner insurrection.

On September 3, Hark Travis, Sam Francis and Nelson Williams were brought to trial. The prosecution was cut and dried, with testimony from an eyewitness, Levi Waller, and Thomas Ridley, the plantation owner who had questioned Hark following his capture. Hark was defended by William C. Parker and pleaded not guilty to the charges. However, it was easily established that Hark was captured while having in his possession the pocketbook of Trajan Doyle, who had been killed on August 22. Hark was sentenced to be hanged on September 9. The state was instructed to pay $450 to the Travis estate for Hark. Other slaves sentenced to death that day included Sam Francis, Nelson Williams, Davy Waller, and the rebellion's other Nat, Edwin Turner's slave, who had left his leader in the woods near the Travis farm on August 23.

In a letter published in Richmond's *Constitutional Whig* on September 6, Jerusalem postmaster Thomas Trezevant told of the slow progress of the trials due to the large number of witnesses who had to be brought in from other sections of the county. To the relief of many Virginians, Trezevant wrote that there was "no good testimony as yet to induce a belief that the conspiracy was a general one." He concluded his letter with an eerie postscript: "Nothing more today. We commence hanging tomorrow."[12]

What of Nat during all this time? Although he could not know that his comrades Hark, Sam, Nat, Davy, and Nelson had been hanged on September 9, he knew that the authorities were still looking for him everywhere. The reward for Nat's capture had swelled to $1,100 by mid-September. As the leaves in Southampton County turned deep red, burnished brown, and golden yellow, as the warmth of September gave way to the chill of October and the ap-

100

proaching winter season, Nat Turner was still nowhere to be found. Everyone in the county wondered where he was. They were very careful to keep their guns handy, and they locked the doors to their farmhouses at night.

Rumors popped up in the newspapers that he had been seen or even caught. On October 4, *The Richmond Enquirer* reported two accounts of "the bandit." One stated that Nat had been captured by "a party of mounted men, who came upon him on the edge of a reed swamp on Nottoway River, about 2 miles [3 km] below Jerusalem." The other report, just as mistaken, said that Nat had been seen on his way to Ohio in Botetourt County, 180 miles (298 km) from Southampton County.

The truth about the fugitive was much less romantic and far simpler. Nat had the good sense to stay put in the area he knew best. Had he wandered around Virginia or attempted to head north, he would have been caught much sooner. In the end, it was only an additional stroke of bad luck that enabled the authorities to finally catch Nat. It all began with a hungry stray dog.

For the most part, Nat stayed hidden during the day and ventured out of his little cave only under cover of darkness. On October 15, a dog wandering near Nat's cave smelled some meat Nat had left inside. The dog crawled into the cave, stole the meat, and was just coming out as Nat made his way back to his hiding place. For some reason he never explained, Nat let the dog go. A few nights later, two slaves were hunting with the dog and passed near Nat's hidden cave. The dog, remembering the meat, led the two blacks to Nat's hiding place and started to bark. Nat had just gone out to stretch his legs. As he returned, he saw the two men. It must have been quite a sight. Here was the dirty and tattered slave leader everyone in the county now called "Preacher Nat" or "The

Prophet" right in front of their eyes. Turner begged them not to betray him. The two slaves fled in obvious terror.

Nat knew that the slaves would give him away, and he left his cave to look for a new place to hide out. Indeed, the two slaves immediately informed their master that they had seen the infamous Nat Turner, and within a day or so over five hundred men were in the area in hot pursuit of the wanted fugitive. They found his hiding place, and inside it a stick Nat had notched to mark the five weeks and six days he had been in hiding. But once again Nat had disappeared.

For the next ten days Nat hid among the stacks of wheat on the plantation of Nathaniel Francis. He may even have thought about surrendering during this time. Since travel by day was impossible, Nat finally tried to get out of the vicinity altogether. But even during the night, Nat found that there was no way he could avoid the white patrols that seemed to be everywhere.

Cold, tired, and hungry, Nat was in great despair. Everything he planned had gone against him. One night he walked to within 2 miles (3 km) of Jerusalem and, only at the last moment, turned around to return to the area of the Travis farm where he continued to hide.

On October 25, Nathaniel Francis was out inspecting his fields when all of a sudden he saw Nat Turner. Francis had been Nat's boyhood playmate, and perhaps Nat felt that because they had known one another all of their lives Francis would treat him fairly. Nat had forgotten that his murdered mistress, Sally Travis, had once been Sally Francis, Nathaniel Francis's sister. As Nat approached the astonished farmer, Francis could see that Nat still had his sword. Armed with his shotgun, Francis aimed and fired. A volley of buckshot passed through the top of Nat's hat and almost tore his head off. Before Francis could reload his gun, the startled Nat grabbed his hat and ran off into the woods.

Now the whites knew that Nat had remained in the vicinity. Within a few hours a search party of fifty men was scouring the area around the Francis property looking for him. Once again, he somehow managed to elude them as they closed in.

On Sunday, October 30, Benjamin Phipps, a local farmer, was out riding on his first patrol. Around noon, as Phipps rode past a clearing in the woods where a number of pine trees had been cut down, the surprised farmer saw something move under the tangle of branches of one of the pines. Suddenly, from under the base of the tree, the face of a man emerged from a small hole that he had dug with his sword. Phipps saw that it was Nat Turner.

Nat was described that day as "torn, emaciated, ragged, 'a mere scarecrow,' still wearing the hat perforated with buckshot." A few days later Nat recalled that Phipps "cocked his gun and aimed at me. I requested him not to shoot and I would give up, upon which he demanded my sword. I delivered it to him." Nat Turner's slave rebellion ended almost exactly where it began. Phipps had found the tired preacher only a mile and a half (2½ km) from the Travis farm.

Turner was taken to the nearby farm of Peter Edwards, where he was confined overnight. Within a few hours a hundred excited people gathered at the Edwards place to get a closer look at the slave preacher who had managed to put fear into the hearts and minds of an entire section of the nation. Soon newspapers all over the South would have bold headlines like that of *The Richmond Enquirer* of November 4: "GEN. NAT TURNER APPREHENDED."

It took four days for news of Turner's capture to reach the desk of Governor John Floyd. Floyd issued the following proclamation:

> We shall attempt to obtain as accurate [an] account
> as possible of this murderous Bandit. We shall
> place it upon record—in order that if any future
> historian should hereafter paint him incorrectly.[13]

The day after his capture, Nat was taken under heavy guard to the county seat in Jerusalem for trial. The trip must have been difficult for Nat because crowds of hostile people screaming for his head met them all along the way. Many whites wanted to lynch Nat on the spot, but the authorities wanted a trial. However, one historian claims that Nat received a public whipping from his guards just to appease the angry mobs. At any rate, Nat arrived in Jerusalem by about one o'clock that afternoon, holding his head high as he and his guards made their way through the throngs of furious townspeople who had gathered to witness the spectacle of the dreaded Prophet being taken to the county jail.

That afternoon Nat stood in front of two judges, James Trezevant and James W. Parker. The officials wanted to hear what Turner had to say, and from the record it appears that Nat was quite willing to talk. A reporter for *The Richmond Enquirer* described Nat that day as "of a darker hue, and his eyes, though large, are not prominent—they are very long, deeply seated in his head, and have a rather sinister expression. A more gloomy fanatic you never heard of."

According to the reporter, Nat spoke that afternoon with amazing candor and appeared to want the court to understand why he did what he did. He spoke of the signs, prayers, and fasting. As those in the court listened intently, Nat spoke of his gifts as a healer and his power to control the weather. He made no attempt to hide his role in the slaughter of the whites. Turner told the still court that the idea of emancipating the blacks had entered his mind only little more than a year before the outbreak took place. Although the reporter pressed Nat for an answer as to how the signs and omens were related to his violent rebellion, Nat's answer did not help to clarify very much. The reporter wrote, "I examined him closely upon this point, he alway [sic] seemed to mystify. He does not, however, pretend to conceal that he was the author of the design, and that he imparted it to five or six others."[14]

The Richmond Whig reported:

Nat seems very humble; willing to answer any questions, indeed quite communicative, and I am disposed to think tells the truth. I heard him speak more than an hour. He readily avowed his motive; confessed that he was the prime instigator of the plot, that he alone opened his master's doors and struck his master the first blow with a hatchet. He clearly verified the accounts which have been given of him. He is a shrewd, intelligent fellow.[15]

Nat told the court that he had never left the county in the two months that had passed since the rebellion and that he "intended to lie by till better times arrived."[16] Nat's trial was set for November 5. He was then escorted by armed guards to the Jerusalem county jail, where he was bound with chains and manacles so that he could not escape. Once in prison, Nat finally learned the fate of his rebellious comrades from several free blacks who were still awaiting trial for their part in the insurrection. They informed Nat that Hark, Sam, Nelson, and Davy Waller had been hanged. A white man asked Nat what he had done with all the money he had stolen from the looted plantations of the murdered whites. Nat angrily replied that he had taken 75 cents and then turned to his free black friends saying, "You know money was not my object."[17]

On November 5, 1831, the Jerusalem County Court of Oyer and Terminer brought Nat Turner to trial. The clerk read the court charges, stating that "Nat alias Nat Turner a negro man slave the property of Putnam Moore an infant charged with conspiring to rebel and making insurrection."

The main witness against Nat was Levi Waller, who had observed him commanding the rebels as they murdered several members of the Waller family. Waller testified that he knew Nat "very well." The next witness, James Trezevant, one of the sitting judges in the case, repeated Nat's testimony of October 31 as well as his confessions to Thomas R. Gray made on November 1.

Nat pleaded not guilty because, as he told his attorney William C. Parker, "he did not feel so." Parker called no witnesses in Nat's defense. Jeremiah Cobb, a wealthy slaveowner who served as the presiding judge, ordered: "Nat Turner! Stand up. Have you anything to say why sentence of death should not be pronounced against you?" Nat answered, "I have not, I have made a full confession to Mr. Gray, and I have nothing more to say." Judge Cobb then sentenced Nat to be hanged on November 11, between 10 A.M. and 4 P.M. Nat was given a value of $375 that the state was required to pay to the estate of the late Putnam Moore.[18]

On Friday, November 11, at around 12 noon, Nat was taken by Sheriff Edward Butts to an old tree near the jail that was used for executions in Jerusalem. In front of a large crowd of people, the sheriff asked Nat if he had anything to say. In a firm voice Nat rejected the offer and told the sheriff that he was ready to die.

According to *The Norfolk Herald*, "He betrayed no emotion but appeared to be utterly reckless in the awful fate that awaited him and even hurried his executioner in the performance of his duty!" From Boston, the abolitionist newspaper, *The Liberator*, reported that Nat "exhibited the utmost composure throughout the whole ceremony.... Not a limb nor a muscle was observed to move." As Nat looked off into the distant skies far above the crowd, the hangman placed the noose around his neck, and he died with quiet dignity.[19]

The attempt to obliterate Nat Turner from the pages of American history began immediately. As William Sidney Drewry wrote in 1900:

The bodies of those executed, with one exception, were buried in a decent and becoming manner. That of Nat Turner was delivered to the doctors, who skinned it and made grease of the flesh. Mr. R. S. Barham's father owned a money purse made of his hide. His skeleton was for many years in the possession of Dr. Massenberg, but has since been misplaced.[20]

7

Bitter Fruits of Rebellion: The Nation Reacts to Nat Turner

She told me that he was a man that was God's man. He was a man for war, and for legal rights, and for freedom.

—Percy Claud Boykins,
recalling in 1969 what his mother
had told him about Nat Turner

No corner of the United States was left untouched by Nat Turner's insurrection. The shots fired in Southampton County had echoed throughout the nation and continued to be heard for generations to come. Panic spread from Virginia to the deepest reaches of the Old South as the master class clamped down on its slaves with what some observers have called "a reign of terror." As Herbert Aptheker has written, "a shiver slid through the South and reached the North."[1]

The immediate painful cost was obvious. Fifty blacks were tried in Southampton County, and twenty-one were hanged. Governor John Floyd intervened in ten other cases, commuting the death sentence handed down by the courts and ruling that the convicted slaves be deported from the country. Blacks were arrested and tried for alleged participation in the rebellion in other parts of Virginia and in nearby North Carolina. A careless statement or a loose gesture of sympathy toward Nat and his rebels was sometimes enough to produce an arrest. As a result, between twenty and thirty more blacks were executed.

In Southampton County, fifty-seven whites had been murdered by the rebels in the space of a few hours. A few more reportedly died of their wounds later. Thus, around sixty whites were killed, and more than two hundred blacks—free men and slaves, guilty and innocent—died in the tumultuous aftermath.

Shocked to the very core of their being by the events in Southampton County, southerners began seeking answers to the Nat Turner rebellion. They frantically sought to place blame on everyone but themselves and their way of life. Many argued that it was no simple coincidence that the Turner insurrection occurred just as militant abolitionism began to appear in the North. Angry southern writers cited William Lloyd Garrison and his abolitionist newspaper as the culprit, while others saw tracts like David Walker's *Appeal* behind Nat Turner's violent outbreak.

Rather than undertaking the difficult evaluation of what was wrong with their own society, the South's leading writers, politicians, and spokesmen began to look for devils everywhere but in their own souls as they linked northern abolitionism with slave rebellions. Virginia's Governor John Floyd was convinced that *The Liberator* was published to promote slave rebellion, and he wondered why there were no laws to punish such "treason." "If this is not checked," he wrote prophetically, "it must lead to a separation of these states."[2]

The truth was that William Lloyd Garrison had condemned violence and force as a means to end slavery. Garrison believed that moral pressure would ultimately convince the South of the evil of slavery. Reacting to the Turner rebellion Garrison wrote: "I do not justify the slaves in their rebellion; yet I do not condemn them, and applaud similar conduct in white men. I deny the right of any people to fight for liberty, and so far am a Quaker in principle."[3]

Even though Garrison and *The Liberator* expressed sorrow at the loss of innocent life in Virginia, with emotions so high in the wake of the Turner revolt, whites were hardly in the mood for any words of sympathy from the very abolitionists they believed guilty of instigating slave rebellion by their antislavery activities and publications.

Writing to Governor James Hamilton, Jr., of South Carolina on November 19, 1831, Governor Floyd blamed Yankee peddlers and northern traders for much of the unrest among the slaves. The Yankees, Floyd charged, told their black friends "that all men were born free and equal—that they cannot serve two masters—that the white people rebelled against England to obtain freedom, so have the blacks a right to do." Meanwhile, Floyd went on, the impulse to revolt was fueled by northern preachers who urged blacks to read and write. Governor Floyd's solution was to recommend that laws be passed "to confine the Slaves to the estates of their masters—prohibit negroes from preaching—absolutely to drive from this State all free negroes."[4]

The hysterical fear that a budding Nat Turner lurked somewhere on the farms or in the cities of the South distinctly expressed itself as southern legislatures hurriedly went into session to discuss the ramifications of the Turner rebellion. The penalty to blacks came quickly in two areas of legislative action. The pressures mounted on southern lawmakers to severely limit the liberties of free southern blacks, while at the same time increase strict regulations on the slaves to ensure that the terrible events in Southampton County were never repeated in the other regions where slavery flourished.

Thus blacks, slave and free, witnessed a torrent of new laws passed after 1831. These laws limited their lives more than at any time in the long-suffering and burdensome history of American slavery.

In 1832, the Delaware state legislature forbade free blacks to keep firearms without a license from a justice of the peace. If more than a dozen free blacks wanted to hold a meeting past 10 P.M., they risked a $10 fine. The state of Maryland forbade the immigration into the state of free blacks after 1831. And if a free black person was caught still living in the state after ten days, a fine of $50 a week was levied. To discourage blacks from sneaking into Maryland, newly arrived blacks were not permitted to be given any type of employment. They were also prohibited from having firearms or "spiritous liquors." In Maryland, after 1831, slaves and free blacks were permitted to have religious services only in the presence of whites.

In 1831, the Georgia State Assembly prohibited slaves from hiring themselves out during their free time, that is, if they had any free time. On December 16, 1831, Tennessee refused to allow free blacks to come into the state and declared that any slave given his or her freedom must immediately leave the state. Tennessee also restricted slaves from meeting "in unusual numbers or at suspicious times and places."

On January 2, 1832, the legislative council in Florida declared that the killing of a slave during a revolt was justifiable homicide and that any person inciting a slave to revolt would be put to death.

In Alabama, anyone who attempted to teach any black person to spell, read, or write could be fined not less than $250 nor more than $500. It became illegal for five male slaves to meet away from their plantation without their master, and after 1832, no free black person was permitted to settle in Alabama under penalty of thirty-nine lashes for the first offense and the penalty of being sold into slavery thereafter.

In 1831–32, the Mississippi Assembly passed a law requiring that all free blacks from sixteen to fifty years of age had to leave the state within ninety days. The authorities allowed persons of "good character" to apply for a license to stay. However, the license, issued only by whites, could be revoked at any time.

When all was said and done, after Nat Turner's rebellion not a single southern state legislature failed to enact new legislation that deeply affected the lives of blacks, both slave and free. Nor did the liberties enjoyed by southern whites escape unscathed in the rush to reinforce black slavery. Freedom of speech and of the press in the South also became a casualty of the Turner insurrection. The State Assembly in Georgia passed a resolution offering $5,000 for the arrest of the publisher or anyone who helped circulate *The Liberator*, as well as "any other paper, circular, pamphlet, letter or address of a seditious character" that incited slaves to rebellion.[5]

For months after the Nat Turner rebellion, South Carolina was frozen in fear of slave uprisings as rumors of revolt spread throughout the state. In Columbia, South Carolina, a vigilance association offered a reward of $1,500 for the arrest of anyone distributing antislavery pamphlets. Two slaves were arrested and convicted for simply saying what they might do if Nat Turner came their way. And in a desperate move to counter the panic that swept Charleston in the wake of the Nat Turner rebellion, the state legislature approved a one-hundred-man cavalry unit, called the Charleston Horse Guard, to protect the city from a slave revolt.

Like other southern states, South Carolina began to wrestle with the question of teaching the slaves to read and write. It was not lost on South Carolinians that Nat Turner was a literate preacher who enjoyed the freedom to move about from one plantation to another so that he could freely organize among the slaves while he preached whatever version of Christianity he happened to choose.

Whitemarsh Seabrook, one of the radical planters in the state who were called "Fireaters" because they defended slavery with great intensity, addressed the South Carolina legislature in 1833. Seabrook urged the passage of a law making teaching a slave to read and write an illegal offense. He argued that anyone who wanted slaves to read the entire Bible was fit for a "room in the Lunatic Asylum." But Seabrook's plea fell on deaf ears that year, and the state senate rejected the bill. Some members argued that it interfered with the "spiritual well being of the slave."

However, the following year, with Nat Turner and the fear of slave revolt still very much on their minds and with the radicals pushing hard, the bill finally passed. Whites convicted of teaching slaves to read or write were liable for a $100 fine and six months in jail. Free blacks convicted of the same offense could be fined $50 and given fifty lashes.

The legislators, curiously, refused to outlaw the teaching of reading and writing to free blacks. There were those in the South Carolina legislature in 1834, however, who still remembered the Denmark Vesey conspiracy. Spurred on by the atrocities committed during the course of the Nat Turner uprising in Virginia, they considered it reckless and dangerous to permit free blacks to learn to read and write. The radical Fireaters attempted to silence virtually all public debate over slavery in South Carolina.[6]

Strangely enough, just the opposite occurred in Virginia, where the public and political debate over slavery seemed to intensify. Instead of closing down the debate over slavery in Virginia, Nat Turner's rebellion helped to trigger it.

Since Thomas Jefferson's death in 1826, there had been hostile rumblings against slavery from the western part of Virginia. The whites who lived in this region had practically no interest in slavery, and their lives were far removed from those of the aristocrats who made up the plantation elite in the Tidewater area. In the aftermath of Nat Turner's revolt, reports filtered into Richmond that whites from the western regions were actually participating in public demonstrations against slavery.

It wasn't that the whites from the mountainous sections of western Virginia loved blacks or thought that slavery was particularly evil. They simply had very few slaves, and to them the Nat Turner rebellion was something that was liable to happen at any time. Why support slavery, some of these whites argued, at the expense of public safety? Thus, their solution to future slave revolts was to liberate Virginia's 470,000 slaves and then get rid of them by colonization abroad.

As 1831 drew to a close, petitions flowed into the Virginia state legislature from all over the state, urging either the removal of all free blacks from the state or the gradual emancipation of the slaves. Owners would be compensated, and the ex-slaves would be colonized somewhere outside the United States.[7]

Even Governor Floyd was torn over the question of slavery. For many years he had been in favor of emancipation followed by colonization. On November 21, only ten days after Nat Turner's execution, Floyd confided in his diary: "Before I leave this Government, I will have contrived to have a law passed gradually abolishing slavery in this State, or at all events to begin work by prohibiting slavery on the

West side of the Blue Ridge Mountains." However, in his long message to the legislature, which was delivered on December 6, 1831, Governor Floyd made no mention whatsoever of freeing Virginia's slaves. Instead, he concentrated on Nat Turner's rebellion by attempting to levy blame for the Southampton revolt on the blacks themselves. As Floyd said,

> The most active among ourselves, in stirring up the spirit of revolt, have been the negro preachers. They had acquired great ascendancy over the minds of their fellows, and infused all their opinions, which had prepared them for the development of the final design.

Governor Floyd blamed the fact that slaves had been freely permitted to take part in religious worship, while their preachers appeared to have other goals in mind. Thus, he recommended that the Virginia legislature revise "all the laws intended to preserve, in due subordination, the slave population of our State."[8]

Although Governor Floyd failed to act decisively, his remarks helped to stimulate what became a major debate over slavery in the Virginia House of Delegates in January and February 1832. First, Thomas Jefferson Randolph, grandson of the third president, offered a plan whereby the state of Virginia would become the owner of every slave when he or she reached the age of twenty-one. Under Randolph's plan, blacks would then be hired out by the state until they could pay for their transportation back to Africa. Soon the debate in the legislature grew heated and intense. Slavery, once a forbidden topic of public debate in the state of Virginia, was now being openly discussed by the elected representatives in the legislature.

Applauding the debate, *The Richmond Enquirer* of February 4, 1832, stated that "nothing else could have prompted them, but the bloody massacre in the month of August." And *The Richmond Whig* added, "Nat Turner and the blood of his innocent victims have conquered the silence of fifty years."[9]

While few members of the state legislature desired to see slavery abolished immediately, a large number were in favor of gradual emancipation. Only a few of the delegates condemned slavery as a violation of human rights and as a moral evil. Most of them were concerned with the effect of slavery on white people or with its negative role in the economic decline that had hit Virginia. Few representatives worried about the destructive effects of slavery on the lives of blacks. Still, there was a debate, and no one who stood up to oppose slavery was threatened with death or violence.

The western delegates warned that future slave revolts would be inevitable. They feared racial warfare in their beloved state unless something was done to hasten freedom for the slaves. However, many spokesmen rose to speak in defense of slavery. They argued that slaves could be controlled by severe laws and insisted that it was a virtuous institution. Some of them even argued that Nat Turner's revolt was not very important because the vast majority of Virginia slaves were loyal to their masters and content with their lives. Their arguments were bolstered by the fact that no westerners could offer a real plan to emancipate the slaves. And so the debate, while interesting, came to nothing. The Virginia legislature's debate over slavery failed because, as John W. Cromwell has written, "no one knew exactly what he wanted, no one came to the legislature with a well-matured plan to remedy the evils, and every man seemed to be governed in his action by his local interests rather than those of the commonwealth." In the end, a resolution for the legislature to act against slavery was defeated. The vote, however, was surprisingly close: 73 to 58.[10]

It is impossible to predict what would have happened if the Virginia state legislature had voted the other way. Some have argued that other state legislatures in the South might have followed and that Nat Turner's revolt impeded the progress of emancipation. Three decades later, on January 1, 1863, President Abraham Lincoln issued the Emancipation Proclamation that finally paved the way for the Thirteenth Amendment to the Constitution, ending slavery in the United States. However, by that time the sectional split between the North and South over slavery had brought on the Civil War, in which more than six hundred thousand Americans lost their lives.

In reality, no one really knows what might have happened if the state of Virginia had emancipated its slaves in 1832. But the historical record is clear. The proslavery forces in Virginia were far more powerful than their opposition. With its rejection of antislavery legislation, the Virginia legislature turned its attention toward restricting the rights of blacks by enacting a series of laws that led to further repression of both slaves and free blacks across the state. Slaves and free blacks were prohibited from holding religious meetings. Free blacks were forbidden from purchasing real estate for a term longer than a year, and they were not allowed to purchase or own firearms. All in all, some twenty new statutes regulating the lives of blacks were added to the books in Virginia.

With memories of Nat Turner fresh in their minds, the Virginia lawmakers worried endlessly about the possibility of future slave revolts. Thus, they turned their backs on talk of emancipation. Instead, they passed new laws to strengthen the militia and the local patrols. When added to the April 1831 law that prohibited the teaching of reading and writing to free blacks and slaves, the restrictive legislation that came in the wake of the Nat Turner rebellion forced the position of blacks to a new historical low in Virginia society.

117

There were a few Virginians who admitted that slavery was truly evil. But still they defended it. General William H. Brodnax of Dinwiddie County had taken part in putting down the Nat Turner rebellion. Yet he had no real sympathy for slavery. "That slavery in Virginia is an evil, and a transcendent evil," Brodnax wrote in January 1832, "it would be idle, and more than idle, for any human being to doubt or deny. It is a mildew which has blighted in its course every region it has touched, from the creation of the world." Yet Brodnax opposed ending slavery because he believed emancipation would "weaken the security of private property, or affect its value."[11]

Following the debate in the Virginia legislature, Governor Floyd invited Professor Thomas R. Dew of William and Mary College to write an analysis of what had taken place. Dew, an avid proslavery sympathizer, produced a long-winded document titled *Dew's Review of the Debates in the Virginia Legislature of 1831 and 1832*. Going back over the Turner rebellion, Dew argued that the conspiracy was the work of only a few slaves. He constructed an elaborate defense of slavery, using history, religion, and political economy.

Playing on the highly charged fears of most white Virginians, Dew's argument came down to race. Turning Thomas Jefferson's ideas on slavery around, Dew maintained that slavery was not evil but good. Slavery, in Dew's mind, was a necessary step in human progress and, more important, a civilizing influence on blacks. Dew assured his readers that they had nothing to fear from their slaves and that Nat Turner was the exception and not the rule. He wrote: "The slave...generally loves the master and his family; and few indeed there are who can coldly plot the murder of men, women, and children; and if they do, there are fewer still who can have the villainy to execute."

For many southerners, Dew's arguments provided the final word on the question of freeing the

118

slaves. "The blacks," Dew insisted, "have now all the habits and feelings of slaves, the whites have those of masters; the prejudices are formed, and mere legislation cannot improve them."[12]

If Nat Turner's insurrection forced many white Virginians to briefly pause, think about, and even debate the evils of slavery, Professor Dew only reinforced their fears and prejudices. With the oppressive new codes safely enacted into law by 1832, white Virginians, no matter how much they might have been worried about a new Nat Turner rising up in the dark of night to cut their throats, were content to return to the way of life they knew and cherished. They were determined to keep slavery no matter what the cost and defended Dew's arguments as the ultimate truth.

In the North, the reaction to Nat Turner was, as might be expected, quite different. The story of the revolt, which received so much newspaper attention in the South, hardly got the coverage or attention it deserved in the northern press. While the abolitionist press saw Nat Turner's uprising as an opportunity to attack the evils of slavery, most northern newspapers were controlled by or affiliated with political parties. Thus, aside from printing an occasional account or two of the rebellion from the Richmond newspapers, the northern press was content with minimum coverage of an event that had rocked every section of the South. *The Albany Argus*, a New York newspaper with close political ties to southern Democrats, was typical of many northern newspapers in its support of the white slaveholding class. In an editorial the paper stated: "If...the rising [by Nat Turner] shall prove to be extensive or formidable, and the danger real, we know with how much alacrity the men of the North will come to the aid of their fellow citizens of the South. The cause is a common one."[13]

While some abolitionists in the North urged the

slaves to continue to rebel and even offered money to help, most of the abolitionists rejected the violence perpetrated by Nat Turner and his followers. The abolitionist response to Nat Turner was, for the most part, self-satisfied. On September 3, 1831, *The Liberator* proclaimed that "What we have so long predicted—at the peril of being stigmatized as an alarmist and declaimer,—has commenced its fulfillment. The first step of the earthquake, which is ultimately to shake down the fabric of oppression…has been made. The first drops of blood, which are but the prelude to a deluge from the gathering clouds, have fallen." On September 24, *The Liberator* added: "We have no room for particulars—not even for comments. So much for oppression! so much for the happiness of the slaves! so much for the security of the South! Where now are our white boasters of liberty?"

However, while white abolitionists carefully measured their reaction to Nat Turner, many northern blacks saw the events in Southampton County in quite a different light. In the 1830s it was still too early for Nat Turner to take on the mantle of a legendary black folk hero. But black abolitionists did not interpret Nat's violent rebellion in negative terms. Some even argued that it was not such a bad thing that Nat Turner fired the first shot in the war against slavery. Writing about what he called "the late tragedy in Virginia" to William Lloyd Garrison on October 20, 1831, the black abolitionist James Forten said, "This insurrection in the south, will be the means of bringing the evils of slavery more prominently before the public, and the urgent sense of danger, if nothing else, will lead to something more than mere hopes."[14]

The intense anxiety generated by Nat Turner's rebellion slowly dissipated. Northerners, preoccupied with tariff debates, industrial growth, and the thorny problem of the rise of militant abolitionism in the 1830s, were content to forget about the revolt in

Southampton County. Southerners attempted to put Nat and his comrades in the back of their minds. After 1832, Virginians and other southerners did their best to avoid any public debate about slavery for fear that discussion might promote slave unrest and encourage the hated abolitionists to even more antislavery activities. Most slaveowners, however, never went to sleep at night without a gun or some weapon close at hand.

By the 1840s, the tough new state slave codes, the reconstituted militias and police power, and an omnipresent military force in the South made any type of organized slave rebellion a virtual impossibility. Governor Floyd retired from office in 1834 with the Southampton insurrection remaining the most important event of his political career. He died in 1837. Aside from a few residents of southeastern Virginia whose lives were directly touched or drastically altered by the Turner revolt, most southerners were more than happy to be rid of the haunting images of an angry army of slaves galloping down the dusty roads of Southampton County and killing every white person in their path.

But try as they would, the white South couldn't rid itself of the ghost of Nat Turner. Old Nat had failed to achieve his goals, but he had earned a place in history. For many years that place was obscured by hatred and fear. Though it seemed, for a long while at least, that history would treat Nat Turner no better than his contemporaries had, his role could not be covered up forever. Sooner or later Nat was destined to emerge from behind the shrouded crypt of southern myth and black folktales and into the brighter light that history could shed on him as a real human being.

8

Nat Turner's Place in History

The history of every people exhibits glory and shame,
heroism and cowardice, wisdom and foolishness,
certainty and doubt, and more often than not these
antagonistic qualities appear at the same moment and
in the same men. The revolutionary task of
intellectuals is, accordingly, not to invent myths, but
to teach each people its own particular contradictory
truth. This historian has never been sure which
lessons can be drawn from the past to serve the future.
Except perhaps one: Until a people can and will face
its own past, it has no future.

—Eugene D. Genovese,
"William Styron before the People's Court,"
In Red and Black, 1971

The first person to open the window of history into Nat Turner's role in the Southampton rebellion was Thomas R. Gray. When Gray, a local Jerusalem attorney, visited Nat Turner in jail on November 1, 1831, the day after his capture, he found the slave leader more than willing to talk about his violent exploits. Nat apparently knew that he was doomed to die and wanted the chance to set the record as straight as possible. Gray recorded his conversation with Nat, and by the end of the month a Baltimore printer published fifty thousand copies of *The Confessions of Nat Turner, the Leader of the Late Insurrection in Southampton, Va. As fully and voluntarily made to Thomas R. Gray.*...

Many southerners strongly disapproved of Gray's decision to circulate Nat's *Confessions,* and the pamphlet was suppressed throughout the South. State and local authorities confiscated and destroyed many copies because they feared that Nat's *Confessions* would lead to new slave unrest and rebellion.

Today most historians accept Gray's version of Nat's confessions as genuine even though Gray was a slaveholder and clearly biased. Gray was the only person to interview Nat before he was executed. He wrote: "If Nat's statements can be relied on, the insurrection in this county was entirely local, and his designs confided but to a few, and these in his immediate vicinity. It was not instigated by motives of revenge or sudden anger, but the results of long deliberation, and a settled purpose of mind."[1]

Gray was convinced that Nat and his men were merciless killers without a shred of remorse for their crimes. He depicts Nat in various places as a "great Bandit," "a gloomy fanatic," and his men as "a fiendish band" and "a band of savages."

Gray clearly betrayed his own prejudices when he wrote:

The calm deliberate composure with which he [Nat] spoke of his late deeds and intentions, the expression of his fiend-like face when excited by enthusiasm, still bearing the stains of the blood

123

> of helpless innocence about him, clothed with
> rags and covered with chains, yet daring to raise
> his manacled hands to heaven, with a spirit soar-
> ing above the attributes of man,—I looked on
> him, and the blood curdled in my veins.[2]

Despite his proslavery feelings and his personal bias, Gray's recorded version of Nat's *Confessions* are the best place to acquire a sense of the real Nat Turner. In many respects, they are the only place to seek the answers to what Nat thought about himself and what he had done. First and foremost, Nat Turner despised slavery and everything that it had done to his people. When Gray asked him to repent, saying, "Do you not find yourself mistaken now?" Nat could only answer, "Was not Christ crucified?"[3] Those whites who knew him may have seen Nat as a bloodthirsty fiend. But Nat saw himself in another light. In his own eyes, he was a martyr spurred on by a deep sense of religious purpose to do the only thing he thought possible at the time by sending the South a clear and bloody message that slavery would have a terrible price.

As the years passed, southerners found that the story of Nat Turner seemed to have a life of its own. No matter how hard they tried to bury Nat or to conceal the tragic events that took place in Southampton County, somehow Nat's revolt stayed alive as his legend grew in black folktales, spirituals, and myth. When John Brown raided Harpers Ferry, Virginia, in 1859 with the intention of arming his abolitionist army of blacks and whites to free the slaves, Nat Turner's revolt once again rose to haunt the mind of the white South. Again a wave of fear, similar to that which followed in Nat Turner's time, swept the region.

Thomas Wentworth Higginson, a white abolitionist who aided John Brown in the 1850s and who became famous as the commander of a black regiment during the Civil War, was the first credible writer to examine the Turner rebellion from a distance. Higginson's essay, "Nat Turner's Insurrection," was published in the widely read *Atlantic Monthly* in August 1861. Higginson portrayed Nat as a militant hero. The slave rebellion's horror was not glossed over, but Higginson saw slavery and the brutal suppression of Nat Turner and his men as an even greater tragedy.

After the Civil War, Nat Turner was once again all but forgotten. For the next thirty-five years, the only scholars to bother with Nat were a few black historians like William Wells Brown, who gave Nat a prominent spot in his books, such as *The Negro in the American Rebellion*. But Brown, a militant black abolitionist who had escaped from slavery himself in 1834, was far more concerned with giving his readers a usable folk hero than he was in getting to the truth. The Nat Turner who emerged in his early writing was a heroic "martyr to the freedom of his race." However, by 1880, Brown accepted the judgment of many observers when he wrote that Nat was "an insane man—made so by slavery."[4]

The first book-length account about Nat Turner was published in 1900 by William S. Drewry, a native of Southampton County. In *The Southampton Insurrection,* Drewry wrote: "The slaves were cared for with the greatest kindness. The white master did not treat his slave as his ox. Slavery was simply domestic servitude, under practically efficient guarantees against ill-treatment." Drewry found the historical Nat to be as elusive as a phantom. He could not understand how a well-treated slave like Nat Turner could possibly want to lead such a bloody rebellion. Drewry completely overlooked the fact that slavery had separated Nat from his wife and children and

125

that Nat was a sensitive man who fully compre-
hended the deadening effects of the brutality of everyday slave life. Drewry claimed that "Cruel treatment
was not a motive for the rebellion.... Nat was a com-
plete fanatic, and believed the Lord had destined him
to free his race."[5]

In 1931, on the centennial anniversary of Nat
Turner's rebellion, the respected black historian
Rayford Logan posed a simple question when he
wrote a short article titled "Nat Turner: Fiend or
Martyr?" Logan's Nat was "a deeply religious, highly
moral Negro slave." Logan wanted 12 million
American blacks to take great pride on November 11,
noting that "on that day one hundred years ago a
black man kept his 'Rendezvous with Death' rather
than live a bondsman." Complaining that Nat Turner
had no monument to commemorate his deed, Logan
saw only a black martyr who died that his people
might one day be free. "Nat Turner," he wrote, "igno-
miniously hanged for seeking liberty, is mentioned
only to be execrated as a bloodthirsty beast."[6]

Still, aside from a few obscure studies in African
American history over the years, Nat Turner was
neglected by students, teachers, and scholars. It wasn't
until the mid-1960s, when Americans found themselves caught up in the full thrust of black America's
long quest for justice and equality during the civil
rights movement, that Nat Turner finally got a second
lease on his historical life. Students and teachers once
again began to explore the famous leader of the
Southampton County slave rebellion of 1831.

Ironically, however, it wasn't a historian who
played the major role in the resurrection of Nat
Turner in the 1960s. It was one of the great American
writers of the post-World War II generation, William
Styron. Styron is a white southerner who had grown
up in the Tidewater area of Virginia not far from

Southampton County, where the Nat Turner rebellion took place.

Styron's 1967 novel, *The Confessions of Nat Turner*, set off an angry debate. His critics, often black, argued that Styron offered readers a negative picture of a man they considered a universally admired African American hero. Much of the criticism against Styron was harsh and often unfair. He was called a "racist" because he was a southern white man who dared to write about a black hero. At times, Styron did portray Nat Turner in an unflattering light, and he did leave out certain vital historical facts. For example, Styron failed to include in his narrative the fact that Nat had a wife and children.

But Styron's novel was a work of fiction. As a novelist, he was free to do whatever he wanted with his characters and to inject his own imagination into his work. Moreover, Styron's portrayal of everyday slave life in the Old South is one of the most remarkable achievements in either history or literature. Few writers or scholars have given us a snapshot in time of southern slavery that compares to the brilliant work of William Styron.

Where do we leave Nat Turner, and how best may we remember him? Many of the writers of his time and historians over the years have labeled him "insane," "a fanatic," and "bloodthirsty." Nat Turner is often lumped with John Brown in any historical discussion about "madmen" who led rebellions against slavery. Echoing Professor Thomas R. Dew, who labeled Nat "a demented fanatic" in 1832, the respected historian Martin Duberman has contended that "the one character trait of Turner that emerges most clearly from those confessions—[is] that he was a religious fanatic of terrifying, perhaps psychotic proportions."[7]

No one in the twentieth century can really be certain if anyone was insane in the nineteenth century. Words like "insane" and "psychotic" are unfair and inaccurate when trying to fit Nat Turner into an understandable and workable historical context. But it would be just as foolish to try to turn Nat Turner into a hero. Responding to the attacks on William Styron, historian Eugene D. Genovese has written that "those who look to history to provide glorious moments and heroes invariably are betrayed into making catastrophic errors in political judgment."[8]

Nat Turner was not a madman and certainly not a saint. The record shows that he was a poor military leader who, on the day before he led his troops into battle, wasn't exactly certain of where they would go. But other great military men and leaders had visions, and no one has ever dared to suggest that they were insane. Chief Crazy Horse of the Oglala Sioux and the famous Sioux medicine man Sitting Bull were two military leaders of their people who often went off into the wilderness to communicate with their God and who claimed to receive visionary messages. The American World War II general George S. Patton, Jr., told many people that he had experienced strange visions of previous lives.

Nat Turner was a man who lived under a vile and oppressive system. In 1831 he decided that he could no longer tolerate the conditions under which he was forced to live as a slave. Thus, he led the bloodiest slave revolt in American history. He sent the white South the important message that no human beings would be content to live forever as slaves. Unfortunately, they chose not to listen.

Nat Turner was a man with the shortcomings and attributes of all men. Neither a hero nor a villain, he fought slavery the only way he thought possible at the time, and for that alone Nat deserves to be remembered. That he chose a violent solution to his dilemma and that so many innocent people, black as well as white, were killed was a great tragedy. But slavery was a violent institution, and it must always be remembered that black Americans endured its violence for over 250 years. In fact, the effects of slavery are still felt in the black community today.

Perhaps it is best to remember Nat in simpler terms. In 1969 seventy-year-old Percy Claud Boykins, a black man who lived about 4 miles (6 km) from the house where Nat had been a slave in Southampton County, Virginia, recalled what his mother had told him about Nat Turner. His words may best describe Nat Turner's place in American history. "She told me," Boykins remembered, "that he was a man that was God's man. He was a man for war, and for legal rights, and for freedom."[9]

Notes

INTRODUCTION
THE SEARCH FOR NAT TURNER

1. Kenneth M. Stampp, *The Peculiar Institution: Slavery in the Ante-Bellum South* (New York, 1956), p. 132.
2. Catherine Clinton, *The Plantation Mistress: Woman's World in the Old South* (New York, 1982), p. 217.
3. Eric Foner, ed., *Nat Turner* (Englewood Cliffs, N.J., 1971), p. 37.
4. Ibid.
5. Samuel Eliot Morison and Henry Steele Commager, *The Growth of the American Republic*, vol. 7 (New York, 1962), pp. 529, 555.
6. Edmund Wilson, *Patriotic Gore* (New York, 1966), pp. 35–37.

CHAPTER 1. NAT TURNER
GROWS UP A SLAVE

1. Stephen B. Oates, *The Fires of Jubilee: Nat Turner's Fierce Rebellion* (New York, 1975), pp. 8–11; and Margaret Mitchell, *Gone With the Wind* (New York, 1940), p. 3.
2. W. J. Cash, *The Mind of the South* (New York, 1941), p. 16.
3. Ibid, pp. 6, 11.

4. *The Confessions of Nat Turner as Told to Thomas R. Gray*, reprinted in Henry Irving Tragle, ed., *The Southampton Slave Revolt of 1831: A Compilation of Source Material* (Amherst, Mass., 1971), p. 306.
5. Ibid, pp. 306–307.
6. John Hope Franklin, *From Slavery to Freedom: A History of Negro Americans* (New York, 1967), p. 59.
7. Oates, *The Fires of Jubilee*, pp. 11, 158.
8. Henry Irving Tragle, ed., *The Southampton Slave Revolt of 1831* (Amherst, Mass., 1991), p. 306.
9. Ibid, p. 307.
10. Oates, *The Fires of Jubilee*, pp. 13–23.
11. Tragle, *The Southampton Slave Revolt of 1831*, p. 308.

CHAPTER 2. NAT TURNER'S WORLD: SLAVERY IN VIRGINIA (1800–1830)

1. John Hope Franklin, *From Slavery to Freedom: A History of Negro Americans* (New York, 1980), pp. 30–33.
2. Ulrich B. Phillips, *American Negro Slavery* (Baton Rouge, La., 1966), p. 77.
3. Fawn Brodie, *Thomas Jefferson: An Intimate History* (New York, 1974), p. 466.
4. Albert Fried, ed., *The Essential Jefferson* (New York, 1963), p. 65.
5. Brodie, *Thomas Jefferson*, pp. 121, 183.
6. Ibid, pp. 183, 220.
7. Robert McColley, *Slavery and Jeffersonian Virginia* (Urbana, Ill., 1964), pp. 125–129, 131.
8. Ibid, pp. 18–19.
9. Franklin, *From Slavery to Freedom*, p. 139.
10. Ibid, p. 137.
11. Kenneth M. Stampp, *The Peculiar Institution: Slavery in the Ante-Bellum South* (New York, 1956), p. 75.
12. Franklin, *From Slavery to Freedom*, p. 139.
13. John W. Blassingame, *The Slave Community: Plantation Life in the Ante-Bellum South* (New York, 1972), p. 39.
14. Robert McColley, *Slavery and Jeffersonian Virginia*, pp. 57–58.
15. Ibid, pp. 60–71.

16. Ibid, p. 65.
17. Fried, *The Essential Jefferson*, p. 556.

CHAPTER 3. TO MAKE THE
MASTER STAND IN FEAR:
SLAVE REBELLIONS IN THE SOUTH

1. Frederick Law Olmsted, *The Slave States*, ed. Harvey Wish (New York, 1959), p. 273.
2. Louis Filler, *The Crusade Against Slavery 1830–1860* (New York, 1960), pp. 14–15.
3. Eugene D. Genovese, *Roll, Jordan, Roll: The World the Slaves Made* (New York, 1972), p. 595.
4. Ibid, p. 594.
5. Herbert Aptheker, *American Negro Slave Revolts* (New York, 1964), pp. 249–250.
6. Ibid, pp. 219–224; also Herbert Aptheker, *Essays in the History of the American Negro* (New York, 1964), pp. 27–31; Ulrich B. Phillips, *American Negro Slavery* (Baton Rouge, La., 1966), pp. 474–475.
7. Fawn Brodie, *Thomas Jefferson: An Intimate History* (New York, 1974), p. 343.
8. Aptheker, *Essays in the History of the American Negro*, p. 41.
9. Richard C. Wade, *Slavery in the Cities: The South 1820–1860* (New York, 1964), p. 228.
10. Ibid, p. 229.
11. Aptheker, *Essays in the History of the American Negro*, p. 41, and *American Negro Slave Revolts*, pp. 269–271.
12. Wade, *Slavery in the Cities*, pp. 229–230.
13. Aptheker, *Essays in the History of the American Negro*, p. 42.
14. Phillips, *American Negro Slavery*, p. 478; and Aptheker, *American Negro Slave Revolts*, p. 271.
15. Wade, *Slavery in the Cities*, p. 233.
16. Aptheker, *American Negro Slave Revolts*, p. 272.
17. Kenneth M. Stampp, *The Peculiar Institution: Slavery in the Ante-Bellum South* (New York, 1956), p. 214.
18. Wade, *Slavery in the Cities*, pp. 240–241.

CHAPTER 4. THE REBELLION TAKES ROOT IN SOUTHAMPTON COUNTY, VIRGINIA

1. William W. Freehling, *Prelude to Civil War: The Nullification Controversy in South Carolina, 1816–1836* (New York, 1968), p. 60.
2. John L. Thomas, ed., *Slavery Attacked: The Abolitionist Crusade* (Englewood Cliffs, N.J., 1965), pp. 6–7.
3. John Hope Franklin, *From Slavery to Freedom: A History of Negro Americans* (New York, 1980), pp. 181–182.
4. Leslie H. Fishel, Jr., and Benjamin Quarles, eds., *The Black American: A Documentary History* (Glenview, Ill., 1970), pp. 173–174.
5. John Hope Franklin, *The Militant South* (Boston, 1964), pp. 80–81.
6. Fishel and Quarles, *The Black American*, pp. 147–152.
7. Stephen B. Oates, *The Fires of Jubilee: Nat Turner's Fierce Rebellion* (New York, 1975), p. 51.
8. Ibid, pp. 27–28.
9. Henry Irving Tragle, ed., *The Southampton Slave Revolt of 1831: A Compilation of Source Material* (Amherst, Mass., 1971), p. 305.
10. Ibid, pp. 308–309.
11. Oates, *The Fires of Jubilee*, pp. 29–31.
12. Tragle, *The Southampton Slave Revolt of 1831*, p. 309.
13. Oates, *The Fires of Jubilee*, p. 39.
14. Tragle, *The Southampton Slave Revolt of 1831*, p. 310.
15. Ibid.
16. Ibid, pp. 310–311.

CHAPTER 5. NAT TURNER'S REBELLION: THE FIRE THIS TIME

1. Henry Irving Tragle, ed., *The Southampton Slave Revolt of 1831: A Compilation of Source Material* (Amherst, Mass., 1971), pp. 193, 202–203.
2. Eric Foner, ed., *Nat Turner* (Englewood Cliffs, N.J., 1971), p. 4.
3. Tragle, *The Southampton Slave Revolt of 1831*, p. 311; and Eric Foner, ed., *Nat Turner*, p. 4.

4. Tragle, *The Southampton Slave Revolt of 1831*, p. 311.
5. Joanne Grant, ed., *Black Protest* (New York, 1968), p. 55.
6. Herbert Aptheker, *Nat Turner's Slave Rebellion* (New York, 1966), p. 47.
7. Tragle, *The Southampton Slave Revolt of 1831*, p. 312.
8. Ibid.
9. Stephen B. Oates, *The Fires of Jubilee: Nat Turner's Fierce Rebellion* (New York, 1975), p. 77.
10. Ibid, p. 79.
11. Tragle, *The Southampton Slave Revolt of 1831*, p. 283; and Oates, *The Fires of Jubilee*, p. 79.
12. Tragle, *The Southampton Slave Revolt of 1831*, pp. 249–252.
13. Oates, *The Fires of Jubilee*, p. 80.
14. Tragle, *The Southampton Slave Revolt of 1831*, p. 313.
15. Ibid, pp. 221–22.
16. Ibid, p. 313.
17. Ibid, pp. 313–314.
18. Ibid, p. 4.

CHAPTER 6. THE FIRE BURNS OUT: ESCAPE, CAPTURE, TRIAL, AND EXECUTION

1. Henry Irving Tragle, ed., *The Southampton Slave Revolt of 1831: A Compilation of Source Material* (Amherst, Mass., 1971), pp. 30, 50–52.
2. Ibid, p. 50.
3. Herbert Aptheker, *Nat Turner's Slave Rebellion* (New York, 1966), p. 53.
4. Tragle, *The Southampton Slave Revolt of 1831*, p. 315.
5. Ibid, pp. 315, 412; and Stephen B. Oates, *The Fires of Jubilee: Nat Turner's Fierce Rebellion* (New York, 1975), p. 95.
6. Tragle, *The Southampton Slave Revolt of 1831*, pp. 48–49; and Aptheker, *Nat Turner's Slave Rebellion*, p. 55.
7. Tragle, *The Southampton Slave Revolt of 1831*, p. 374.
8. Ibid, pp. 11, 69, 374.
9. Oates, *The Fires of Jubilee*, pp. 100–101.
10. Tragle, *The Southampton Slave Revolt of 1831*, pp. 92–93.

11. Ibid, pp. 420–421; also see Eric Foner, ed., *Nat Turner*, (Englewood Cliffs, N.J., 1971), p. 13.
12. Oates, *The Fires of Jubilee*, p. 103; and Tragle, *The Southampton Slave Revolt of 1831*, pp. 72–73, 174, 232.
13.Tragle, *The Southampton Slave Revolt of 1831*, pp. 316, 345.
14. Ibid, pp. 133–134, 137.
15. Foner, *Nat Turner*, pp. 31–32.
16. Ibid.
17. Oates, *The Fires of Jubilee*, p. 120.
18. Tragle, *The Southampton Slave Revolt of 1831*, pp. 221–223, 318–319.
19. Foner, *Nat Turner*, pp. 35–36; Tragle, *The Southampton Slave Revolt of 1831*, p. 140.
20. William Styron, *The Confessions of Nat Turner* (New York, 1966), p. 429.

CHAPTER 7. BITTER FRUITS OF REBELLION: THE NATION REACTS TO NAT TURNER

1. Herbert Aptheker, *Nat Turner's Slave Rebellion* (New York, 1966), p. 57.
2. Henry Irving Tragle, ed., *The Southampton Slave Revolt of 1831: A Compilation of Source Material* (Amherst, Mass., 1971), pp. 256, 286.
3. Eric Foner, ed., *Nat Turner* (Englewood Cliffs, N.J., 1971), p. 83.
4. Tragle, *The Southampton Slave Revolt of 1831*, pp. 275–276.
5. Aptheker, *Nat Turner's Slave Rebellion*, pp. 74–83.
6. William W. Freehling, *Prelude to Civil War: The Nullification Controversy in South Carolina, 1816–1836* (New York, 1968), pp. 334–335.
7. Foner, *Nat Turner*, pp. 7–8; and Stephen B. Oates, *The Fires of Jubilee: Nat Turner's Fierce Rebellion* (New York, 1975) p. 135.
8. Tragle, *The Southampton Slave Revolt of 1831*, pp. 261, 432–435.
9. Ibid, pp. 153, 381; Foner, *Nat Turner*, p. 8.
10. Foner, *Nat Turner*, pp. 8–9; and Tragle, *The Southampton Slave Revolt of 1831*, pp. 382–384.

11. Foner, *Nat Turner*, pp. 108–110.
12. Ibid, p. 123; and George M. Frederickson, *The Black Image in the White Mind: The Debate on Afro-American Character and Destiny, 1817–1914* (New York, 1971), pp. 44–45.
13. Foner, *Nat Turner*, pp. 77–78.
14. Ibid, pp. 80, 83, 85.

CHAPTER 8. NAT TURNER'S PLACE IN HISTORY

1. Henry Irving Tragle, ed., *The Southampton Slave Revolt of 1831: A Compilation of Source Material* (Amherst, Mass., 1971), pp. 304–305.
2. Ibid, pp. 303–305, 347; and Eric Foner, ed., *Nat Turner*, (Englewood Cliffs, N.J., 1971), p. 37.
3. Tragle, *The Southampton Slave Revolt of 1831*, p. 310.
4. Foner, *Nat Turner*, p. 141.
5. Ibid, pp. 152–153.
6. Ibid, pp. 162–165.
7. Martin Duberman, *The Uncompleted Past* (New York, 1969), p. 220.
8. Eugene D. Genovese, *In Red and Black: Marxian Explorations in Southern and Afro-American History* (New York, 1971), p. 201.
9. Tragle, *The Southampton Slave Revolt of 1831*, p. 13.

Bibliography

NAT TURNER

Aptheker, Herbert. *American Negro Slave Revolts*. New York: International Publishers, 1964.

Aptheker, Herbert. *Nat Turner's Slave Rebellion*. New York: Grove Press, 1966.

Clarke, John Henrik, ed. *William Styron's Nat Turner: Ten Black Writers Respond*. Boston: Beacon Press, 1968.

Foner, Eric, ed. *Nat Turner*. Englewood Cliffs, N.J.: Prentice-Hall, 1971.

Gray, Thomas R. *The Confessions of Nat Turner, The Leader of the Late Insurrection in Southampton, Va. As fully and voluntarily made to Thomas R. Gray....* Baltimore: Thomas R. Gray, 1831.

Oates, Stephen B. *The Fires of Jubilee: Nat Turner's Fierce Rebellion*. New York: Harper and Row, 1975.

Styron, William. *The Confessions of Nat Turner*. New York: Random House, 1966.

Tragle, Henry Irving, ed. *The Southampton Slave Revolt of 1831: A Compilation of Source Material*. Amherst, Mass.: University of Massachusetts Press, 1971. Contains a copy of Gray's *Confessions*.

SLAVERY

Blassingame, John W. *The Slave Community: Plantation Life in the Ante-Bellum South*. New York: Oxford University Press, 1972.

Elkins, Stanley M. *Slavery: A Problem in American Institutional and Intellectual Life*. Chicago: University of Chicago Press, 1959.

Genovese, Eugene D. *Roll, Jordan, Roll: The World the Slaves Made*. New York: Random House, 1972.

McColley, Robert. *Slavery and Jeffersonian Virginia*. Urbana, Ill.: University of Illinois Press, 1964.

Phillips, Ulrich B. *American Negro Slavery*. Baton Rouge, La.: Louisiana State University Press, 1966.

Stampp, Kenneth M. *The Peculiar Institution: Slavery in the Ante-Bellum South*. New York: Alfred A. Knopf, 1967.

Wade, Richard C. *Slavery in the Cities: The South 1820–1860*. New York: Oxford University Press, 1964.

GENERAL WORKS IN AFRO-AMERICAN AND SOUTHERN HISTORY

Cash, W. J. *The Mind of the South*. New York: Vintage Books, 1941.

Franklin, John Hope. *From Slavery to Freedom: A History of Negro Americans*. New York: Alfred A. Knopf, 1980.

Genovese, Eugene D. *In Red and Black: Marxian Explorations in Southern and Afro-American History*. New York: Random House, 1971.

Genovese, Eugene D. *The World the Slaveholders Made*. New York: Vintage Books, 1971.

Index

Deslondes, Charles, 43
Dew, Thomas R., 118–119,
127
Doyle, Henry, 81, 82
Doyle, Trajan, 80, 100
*Dred: A Tale of the Dismal
Swamp*, 9–10
Drewry, William Sidney,
107, 125–126
Drury, Edwin, 86
Duberman, Martin, 127

Edwards, Peter, 84, 103
Eppes, Richard, 95–96, 99

Floyd, John, 57, 83, 84,
103–104, 109, 110, 114,
118, 121
Forten, James, 57, 120
Francis, Lavinia, 81, 82
Francis, Nathaniel, 66, 80,
81, 82, 102
Francis, Salathul, 76–77
Francis, Sam, 66, 81–82, 100,
105
Francis, Will, 66, 71–76,
81–82, 94
Franklin, Benjamin, 25
Franklin, John Hope, 15,
30–31
French, James L., 99

Gabriel Plot, Virginia (1800),
39, 43–48
Garnet, Henry Highland, 38
Garrison, William Lloyd,
55–58, 109, 110, 120
Genovese, Eugene D., 42,
122, 128
Gray, Thomas R., 8, 9, 62, 99,

106, 122–124
*Growth of the American
Republic, The,* 9

Hamilton, James Jr., 110
Harris, Howell, 80
Harris, Newit, 84, 93
Higginson, Thomas
Wentworth, 70, 124–
125

Jackson, Andrew, 58, 97
Jefferson, Thomas, 21,
23–27, 29, 36–37, 44, 47,
48, 114

Lee, Shepherd, 88
Liberator, The, 56, 57, 107,
109, 110, 112, 120
Lincoln, Abraham, 117
Logan, Rayford, 126
Louisiana revolt (1811),
42–43

McColley, Robert, 28
Middleton, Arthur, 86
Mifflin, Warner, 26
Monroe, James, 44, 45, 46, 47
Moore, Putnam, 65, 76
Moore, Sally, 65, 66
Moore, Thomas, 61, 65, 78
Morison, Samuel Eliot, 9

*Negro in the American
Rebellion, The,* 125
Newsome, Sarah, 78
Norforlk Herald, The, 106–107

Olmsted, Frederick Law,
39–40

About the Author

Martin S. Goldman grew up and went to school in Philadelphia, Pennsylvania. An author, teacher, and journalist, Mr. Goldman has taught African-American history at Clark University, Rutgers University, and Boston University, where he lectures at Metropolitan College. From 1985 to 1989 he was editor of *This Week* and *The Boston Ledger*. Many of his political articles have appeared in *The Boston Globe*, *The Boston Herald*, and *The Boston Phoenix*. From 1987 to 1990 he was the political columnist for *Bostonia Magazine*.

Mr. Goldman received his B.S. and M.A. from Temple University, Philadelphia, and completed his Ph.D. requirements at Clark University in Worcester, Massachusetts.

Mr. Goldman is currently working on a book about the Democratic party in Massachusetts. He lives in the peaceful town of Sudbury, Massachusetts.